Scientific
Charles
Recalls
A
Poetic
Stevenson

Charles A. Stevenson

Grosvenor House
Publishing Limited

The right of Charles A. Stevenson to be identified as the author of this
work has been asserted in accordance with Section 78
of the Copyright, Designs and Patents Act 1988

The book cover is copyright to Charles A. Stevenson

This book is published by
Grosvenor House Publishing Ltd
Link House
140 The Broadway, Tolworth, Surrey, KT6 7HT.
www.grosvenorhousepublishing.co.uk

A CIP record for this book
is available from the British Library

ISBN 978-1-80381-615-9

For May

SCRAPS
MEMORIES OF LOTHIAN LIFE &
ROBERT LOUIS STEVENSON

By his cousin
Charles A. Stevenson

Hon. Member of the Institution of Civil Engineers

Charles Stevenson inventor of:

- the flashing light for buoys now used the entire world over
- the leader submarine cable
- the equiangular prism for making lights shine more brightly
- the inaccessible fog gun started and stopped by wireless
- the combination of hypo radiant & 1st order apparatus of lights for maximum candlepower
- the electrically driven fog signal using submarine cable as at Platte Fougere, Guernsey
- apparatus for using acetylene explosions as a fog signal
- the first to transmit voice across space by the broadcast of speech.

ORIGINALLY TRANSCRIBED & EDITED BY E.M. YEOMAN M.B.E.

Charles A Stevenson

Contents

Family Context	ix
Introduction – How This Book Came About	xi
Robert Stevenson – The First of the Stevenson Engineers	1
Robert's Volunteering	5
Heredity	6
The Heredity of Women	8
Mrs Stevenson Enjoys her Sons' Fun	12
Louis – A Quick Introduction	13
Louis' Enjoyment of Life	17
Thoughts of Childhood in Verse	19
Louis' Dog Coolin	25
Thomas Stevenson – The Boy's Father	26
Louis in Prison – The Snowball Riot	28
Louis' Literary Work Devoid of Boasting	29
Iona and Dhu Heartach	31
Alan and the Stevenson Gaiety of Spirit	33
Muckle Flugga and North Unst	37
Louis' Playground	40
The Pavilion on the Links	41
Dirleton Quicksand	43
North Berwick and the Islets	45
Damming the Eel Burn	52
The Black Rock	53
Boating	55
Louis – A Lover of Soap Bells	57
Golf	59
Kite Flying	61

Catriona	62
Summer Quarters at North Berwick	65
Louis at North Berwick	67
Trip to Italy and a Missed Ball	72
Louis' Other Cousins	74
Edinburgh in the 19th Century	77
The Edinburgh Skating Club	84
The Bugle Call and its Revival	87
A Comparison of Homelife	88
25 Royal Terrace, Edinburgh	91
Melville Street – Another Stevenson Home	95
Louis as a Companion	100
From a Railway Carriage	102
And More of Louis	104
Louis' Theatricals	106
America	108
Preface to Louis' Scots Poems	109
At North Berwick Law	112
The Speculative Society	123
A Dinner Speech	124
The Royal Society of Edinburgh	127
In Narrow Waters	128
Louis' Ladder of Fame	129
D. Alan Stevenson	132
The Pharos of Alexandria	133
A Final Thought	135
Appendix	136

Family Context

The family tree as drawn by Charles, showing just three great grandchildren at that time. Charles' writing was shaky by then, as can be seen in this simplified family tree. It ignores many including Robert's son Alan.

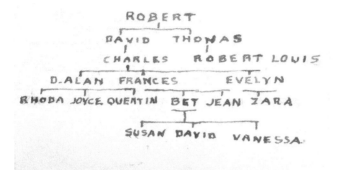

The SCRAPS manuscript opened with a copy of a distant landscape watercolour captioned.

EDINBURGH, with Arthur's Seat, the Calton Hill and the Castle. The Home of the Stevenson family and it still is so.

Charles showed a significant interest in the topography of the land both in and around Edinburgh and East Lothian in what he wrote, which is reflective of his professional background.

Charles and his wife Margaret 'Meta' Sherriff.

Charles and his daughter Frances, looking somewhat nervous, on a visit to Platte Fougere, Guernsey, from a glass plate photograph.

Introduction – How This Book Came About

World War Two was ending and my grandmother, May Yeoman (nee Evelyn Mary Stevenson), needed a new focus in her life. She had spent the best part of five years doing her bit for morale but now she was ready for a new challenge.

Her father, Charles Stevenson – known within the family as 'Pops', was in his 90s. Although Charles was still of sound mind, he was losing his sight and could no longer concentrate his efforts on engineering issues. He was housebound and was cared for at home by May and a nursing assistant.

Charles was determined to make a record of his early life often spent in the company of one of Britain's greatest 19th century writers – his cousin Robert Louis Stevenson (RLS).

RLS, known as 'Louis' within the family, was an only child and while the Stevenson cousins were growing up, he spent a lot of time together with Charles and his sisters, particularly when both sets of families spent their summer months at North Berwick in East Lothian.

Charles was keen to record memories of his youth, particularly those involving his cousin. It was now or never, and he could see his daughter would soon be at a loose end. It wasn't a case of a degree of cunning on his behalf, but the hand of cards that fate had dealt them both. So, for a few short years after World War II my grandmother spent hours acting as both scribe and typist for her father.

It is not entirely clear what Charles' original intention was for this work. It is a tri-emeritus record of his thoughts and memories of Edinburgh, North Berwick and the Stevensons. However, it is clear he made a significant effort to recall what he could of RLS from their time together nearly 70 years earlier, within a family context. It appears he was particularly annoyed by some of the inaccuracies in a biography written a few years before he prepared his notes, especially when referring to the early years of RLS's life.

Charles' manuscript document, known only as *SCRAPS*, was compiled by May according to his instructions. This included his pencil and ink corrections or clarifications and a little subsequent editing. Some changes have now been made to the order of items from the original manuscript to follow a more chronological flow. I felt it would be beneficial to make some allowance for the use of more modern language. Most of the photographs are those belonging to Charles and were taken around 150 years ago.

May had been instructed that there would be a frontispiece. This was still in a rough draft, written in note form on a piece of paper from the King George and Queen Elizabeth Officers' Club, of which May was the Secretary during the Second World War. No mention was made of the 23 lighthouses he was responsible for building.

Maybe because of his longevity, Charles did not get the obituary he deserved, providing enough merit for his achievements. Charles' numerous research and development contributions to engineering practice, which involved optics, electricity and radio, harnessed to furthering maritime convenience and safety, were in the very finest tradition of his profession. Charles was the only Stevenson to become a member of the Institution of Electrical Engineers, being elected a Companion in 1929. As has been acknowledged by others he may indeed have been the most inventive of the Stevenson engineers.

I was born two years after Charles' death, however I stayed with my grandmother, May, at Douglas Crescent on numerous occasions over a period of 20 years. I was told many stories by her and her brother Alan. One routine that operated like clockwork were the Sunday morning visits from Alan to call on May for a coffee and chat. Below is a photograph of May and Alan taken in the early 1960s.

Roderick Groundes-Peace
Great grandson of Charles

May and Alan at Waverley Station, Edinburgh in the 1960s.

Robert Stevenson – The First of the Stevenson Engineers

Much is written about Robert Stevenson's fame from his project of the Bell Rock Lighthouse. Perhaps there is less public knowledge of his civil engineering work within Edinburgh. In the early 19th century, there was an integrated plan of improvements for the city, to include opening up the unique view of Calton Hill from Princes Street and the view of Arthur's Seat and the Old Town of Edinburgh from the highway that Robert designed and made between Princes Street and Abbey Hill. This new highway involved the removal of houses to the east of Princes Street; a crossing for the ravine where the Waterloo Bridge now stands; the cutting through of a graveyard in Waterloo Place following the line of the road; the erection of a rustic retaining wall opposite where the present high school is situated and the enclosure of a new burial ground. The original Stevenson burial ground was in the centre of what is now Waterloo Place and its site had to be shifted to a New Calton burial ground when the road was constructed. Robert's conception of such a comprehensive scheme was bold and was much admired by the subsequent engineers in the family. Sadly, for Louis the merit of the civil engineering achievement by his grandfather seems not to have been fully grasped or understood.

The panoramic improvements to the City of Edinburgh by Robert exemplify the cleverness of the man who designed the highway and who saw no difficulty in carrying a road over a ravine below and in forming a high retaining wall, as well as undertaking heavy rock excavations. His strength of character was necessary as this project had to be carried out despite extensive public opposition.

Portrait of Robert Stevenson with Turner's oil painting of the Bell Rock Lighthouse in the background.

The Bell Rock Lighthouse, from an engraving of Turner's painting.

Robert Stevenson is best remembered for the Bell Rock Lighthouse, perhaps one of the most famous lighthouses in the world, on the difficult Bell Rock, off Arbroath.

A devastatingly dangerous obstruction to Scotland's eastern coast, Bell Rock becomes submerged at high tide and typically claimed six ships every winter until the lighthouse was built.

The Bell Rock Lighthouse was conceived, designed and created by Robert Stevenson and built by the firm of Thomas Smith, Stevenson's father-in-law and the first Engineer to the Northern Lighthouse Board.

During the construction of the lighthouse, the bell shown in the photograph below was rung to warn the masons to seek shelter when the tide was rising.

The cost of the lighthouse was £61,331, which in the construction costs of 2020 would equate to more than £300 million.

When the construction of the lighthouse was completed on 1st February 1811, the tower contained more than 2,000 tons of stone and the light stood 104 feet above the foundation.

The lighthouse was immortalised by the words of Sir Walter Scott when he visited it with Robert Stevenson in 1814:

Far in the bosom of the deep
O'er these wild shelves my watch I keep
A ruddy gem of changeful light
Bound on the dusky brow of Night
The Seaman bids my lustre hail
And scorns to strike his tim'rous sail

This verse by Scott was inscribed in the lighthouse visitor's book, after he had paused for merely a few moments. He described the tower as being crowned by Stevenson's red and white revolving light.

In the biography *The Life of Robert Stevenson,* the author describes the rock and the foundation pit for the tower:

'This pit and rock are flooded over twice a day by tide wave with 13 feet of water.

Sea tangle and seaweed and no beach –

No place for men most of the day.'

Finally, to understand why the need for this lighthouse was so important for the safety of shipping, the following quote from Stoddard's Remarks on Scotland: and its waters gives a clue to us:

"In the North Sea there lyes a great hidden rock called Inchcape, very dangerous for navigation. It is reported in old times, upon the saide rock there was a bell, fixed upon a tree or timber, which rang continually, being moved by the sea, giving notice to the saylers of the danger. This bell or clocke was put there and maintained by the Abbott of Aberbrothok and being taken down by sea pirates, a year therefore he perished upon the rocke, with ship and goodes, in the righteous judgement of God".

4

Robert's Volunteering

From David Stevenson's book on the life of Robert Stevenson (1878) there is an extract recorded by Robert himself:

> "After my return from the Pentland Skerries in 1794, I enrolled myself as a private in the 1st Regiment of Edinburgh volunteers, raised as the local Defenders of our Firesides against the threatened invasion by the French and served about five years in the ranks of the corps. However, when the war became hot and invasion was fully expected, other corps of volunteers were embodied, when I was promoted to be lieutenant in the Princess Charlotte's Royals and later Captain of the Grenadier Company."

Robert spent 13 years as an active volunteer and on his resignation was made an honorary Captain, a title he held until he died.

The question might be asked as to why Louis did not follow the noble example of his grandfather, who had become a volunteer back in 1794 when invasion by the French was imminent and remained a volunteer until the time of erecting the Bell Rock Lighthouse, which was deemed a work of national importance. Louis a confirmed defender of our 'Fireside' could not realistically be described as a man of valour, romance yes. Besides there was no invasion threat during his lifetime.

Heredity

I am often asked how far heredity affected Louis. Our great-grandfather, Thomas Smith, was a ship owner and underwriter. He was a man of most extraordinary mechanical invention in both optical and building ways; his architecture was pre-eminent. His office of ship-owning was south of Tron Church in Edinburgh. Behind the office he carried out his optical work until he moved into larger premises at Greenside. Perhaps now is the time to explain that Thomas was Jean's father as well as becoming Robert's stepfather upon marrying Robert's mother when she was widowed. Today it might seem a little unusual that Robert and Jean married but it was considered less so then.

Louis' grandfather (Robert Stevenson of Bell Rock fame) had both a strong intellect and very considerable mathematical knowledge, which was of great service in his designing of his lighthouse, enabling him to select the best curve for the profile of the tower as well as other features.

It can never be said therefore that Louis' intellect 'came out of the blue' as he had most knowledgeable and skilled ancestors. As an aside, it was at an early time in his life that Louis dropped the name Balfour, cut the letter from his initials RLBS and he had changed his name from Lewis to Louis.

As instances of possible heredity, we should make mention of Robert Stevenson's very perfect choice of words. This brilliant feature of Robert Stevenson's writings is apparent in his diaries, books, letters and reports all bearing witness to his genius. In all his work and civil engineering constructions, the practicality and usefulness of design is visible; the hallmark of a good architect.

Another instance, where Louis seemed perhaps to be gifted with the same likings as Robert was in their shared keen interest in bird life. Robert Stevenson kept an eagle in captivity in his garden in Edinburgh for many years. He also had a great auk on board his ship for a while, no doubt intending to bring it home. The bird was allowed to enjoy itself by swimming in the sea attached by a cord. One day through someone's carelessness the bird managed to escape and was never seen again. Curiously Robert found a dead auk while at sea in the Bristol Channel. This was the last of the great auks seen in this country. I have been asked what a great auk is like, and I tried to sketch the interesting bird with its strong beak and jaws. Sadly, my drawing no longer exists.

A bird fancier, knowing that Robert had kept an eagle for years, brought him a macaw. However, after telling Robert of its beauty and virtues the man was told, 'My good man, take your bird away. I would not give a farthing for a cartload of them!'

Robert, like Louis, having always been interested in birds, gave an account of the most exceptional storm he ever experienced at sea:

> There seemed to have been no division between the heavens above and the sea below. The seagulls were driven off the sea blown away powerless among the mingled air and water.

Finally, Louis had a great flair for horseback riding for mere pleasure. Whether his grandfather enjoyed riding as much as Louis, I do not know. Robert used horses frequently in his business as a road and bridge engineer, sometimes going on horseback journeys lasting many days both in England and in Scotland. Louis continued to ride horses for pleasure until the last day of his life.

The Heredity of Women

Mater Triumphans (Motherhood Supreme):

Son of my woman's body, you go, to the drum and fife,
To taste the colour of love and the other side of life-
From out of the dainty the rude, the strong from out of the frail,
Eternally through the ages from the female comes the male.

The ten fingers and toes and the shell-like nail on each,
The eyes blind as gems and the tongue attempted speech;
Impotent hands in my bosom and yet they shall wield the sword!
Drugged with slumber and milk, you wait the day of the Lord.

Infant bridegroom, uncrowned king, unanointed priest,
Soldier, lover, explorer, I see you nuzzle the breast.
You that grope in my bosom shall load the ladies with rings,
You, that came forth through the doors, shall burst the doors of kings.

RLS

It is a marked feature of Scottish life to be interested in one's ancestral lineage and Louis, from the time he was a boy, was no exception. He was always keen to add to his knowledge of what was inherited from his kith and kin. In his wondrous poem *Mater Triumphans* he points out how strong woman's power was regarding heredity, especially in the line 'Eternally through the ages from the female comes the male' and there is a sketch of his grandmother, with Louis mirrored from his very soul unto his fingertips.

Louis was always very enthusiastic about the inheritance of genes. He was under no misapprehension that the genes and inherited characteristics only came from the male side.

It had been remarked that both grandmother and grandson were armoured throughout life with that 'Gaiety of Spirit' being the mainspring of both their lives. Louis has written of this and now is included by me in this introduction to my little volume. It remains a marked feature of the Stevenson family.

Jean (Robert Stevenson's wife and Louis' grandmother) was a handsome woman. The very fact that there are two oil paintings of the good lady, as well as a miniature of her, all point to her being a woman of note. She had a kind, thoughtful face with lovely dark hair and a finely modelled figure. One of the artists for whom she sat must have been a man of keen insight as he not merely picked out her character, but he managed to bring them to life – her kindly face and beautiful hands, very capable of sewing fine thread. In each of Mrs Stevenson's pictures her hair and dress differ, showing she kept herself in the height of fashion.

It is evident she expertly maintained a superior household with a family consisting of four sons and one daughter as well as herself and Robert. This was not a single-handed operation as in their large house she had a cook, a table maid, a housemaid and a nurse. The nurse was called Aggie. When I knew her, she was too frail to continue working but she was retained by my father. Catherine, known as Cashie, was the nurse in my father's house. In Louis's house the nurse was Cummy. All three of these women spoke the same tongue, Lowland Scots and not English. Cashie and Cummy were close friends and many a time in the evening Cummy was in our nursery as a visitor, sometimes also bringing Louis.

At the time of her marriage to Robert, Jean brought considerable goods and a wealth of family linen, together with elaborate woven fabrics as part of her dowry. She merited the confidence of all and had a large court of flatterers and friends, which Louis perhaps rather unkindly referred to as 'the parasites'.

Mrs Stevenson must have looked smart and imposing when she went out to make return calls on her numerous lady friends. She had a formidable presence with her ivory handled walking stick and five feet of gold chain around her neck, all set off by a broad brimmed hat. I presume that she carried her embossed gold watch and vinaigrette (smelling salts bottle), as well as her distinctive pearl brooch. She had a concealed under-pocket hidden within her skirt where she could carry money as well as 'goodies' for children, enabling her to dispense as she wished while on her way. She was full of fun and so were her boys, especially Alan who was forever making up amusing rhymes about family matters – enough to make a cow smile! It is a thousand pities I had not written down these lines from Alan. I was told of them by my father, and I am sure they would have made you as readers laugh, although you be not of the common herd!

Jean, Robert's wife and her daughter Jane would have been very displeased if I had not included a picture showing the two women dressed not for 'battle' but for the 'breeze' with their French mantels, thick enough to keep them warm should they have met with a storm, together with rain and spray in the small boat. Jean's note explained:

> "These striped mantels were ample shelter for hats and all in a trice; we could be ready to sit down to the most sumptuous luncheon that any battleship could provide. Then as to the millinery our hats with ribbons – so sweet – are of the latest fashion and just brought straight over from Paris in a huge box by the head of the House. What a dear he is! With the rest of the two angels' robes and appurtenances I fear to tread. Sufficient, that it was a mid-summer morning in a small boat 50 miles from home in the North Sea and 12 miles from land – how nice – with the family nurse Aggie, with us in the bow of the boat but alas with a face betokening her discomfiture! Poor old soul. "

Aggie would have had Louis' sympathy as he was also afflicted by seasickness, even with the merest breathing of the ocean.

> The boat is guided by three oars; the man at the bow aiding with his left in turning the boat's bow rapidly to the rock to affect a landing. It is half flood tide and consequently there is a rapid tide current past the rock which had to be countered with a good strong pull of the oar.

Louis' grandmother and aunt go a-boating more than a century ago – 'Heigh ho – and a bottle of fun!'

Although not explained by Charles there can be little doubt this print enlargement depicts a landing on the Bell Rock at the time of the lighthouse being built. As the rock is 12 miles away from the shore, it must be assumed the rowing boat would have been launched from a ship at anchor nearby.

Mrs Stevenson Enjoys Her Sons' Fun

Three of Jean's boys were on a trip in the North of Scotland with their father, after which they returned with a tale. The boys had been sitting in church, occupying the front seat of a gallery only a few yards from the minister and the precentor, as the church was small. Alan, as was his want, likened the appearance of the precentor's shaggy locks to dried seaweed. Inwardly no doubt Alan had a few seconds of silent laughter but not wishing to keep all the fun to himself whispered along the line, 'Isn't his hair like dried seaweed.' That of course was the end of all things – first one boy disappeared from the gallery with the pangs of constrained bursting laughter, soon followed by the other in a similar condition and finally by Alan, as solemn as a judge I presume! They knew that their father, from his seat in the middle of the church, would have noticed their absence and hence they wondered what 'the Dickens' their fate would be. Robert, at the end of the service, joined them outside the church and asked what had really happened and on hearing from Alan the cause, he merely said, 'And to tell the truth I had a good laugh myself, but you boys must learn to control yourselves!'

Louis – A Quick Introduction

Speaking out, saying what he was thinking – that was Louis. Everything else was as nothing.

God grant to me Courage
Gaiety of Spirit and
Tranquillity of Mind

Go, little book and wish to all
Flowers to the garden
Meat in the hall.

RLS

May the same good luck which the nurse showers on the child she holds, be the welcome given by the public to this little volume of mine.

Charles A Stevenson

I have often been asked to describe Louis. In an attempt to satisfy those who are curious as to the details of Louis' appearance perhaps it is helpful to start with a few remarks.

My cousin Louis had eyes, gifted to few, that it seemed to allow one to look right into his soul. The eyes of some may have the large beautifully coloured iris and the lovely pearly white of the sclera. Others might have eyelashes of superb length and curvature set in most delicately coloured eyelids, eyebrows of lovely shape and texture, yet fail to have the property which Louis' eyes seemed to possess. I truly felt I could glance right into his very being.

Louis' hands were beautiful like his grandmother's, being delicately shaped with tapered fingers, a feature much admired by women. Perhaps for a man his hands were less well suited to grasping a cricket bat or retain hold of a football or rifle, not having the firmness and force more expected of men. That is not to say his hands were not clever, say in adjusting the likes of neatly and quickly rolling cigarettes. As a young boy he smoked, and he carried on smoking cigarettes throughout school life. However, he was strong enough to go rowing or canoeing in the *Aerthusa* or horseback riding.

Louis was not tall, yet he was above average height. He was not massively built nor ready to enter upon any rough and tumble game, or boy's fight. His build was slight and erect which gave him graceful movement. He walked steadily and well, being nimble of foot. As I have said his hands were not of the muscular class, nor evident of a strong grip. Although Louis was not of a particularly strong type, he was no weakling. In some ways he was just an ordinary type of boy and youth.

His hair was not curly, yet he had noticeably and distinct long waves. The hair was neither black, nor was it in the least degree even dark from the roots as the public naturally thinks. Louis was not like his cousin Bob who did have black hair and a black moustache. Photographs of Louis show that he had a great wealth of hair but incorrectly give the impression of his hair being black, jet black. This is not right, which is very evident in the case of Louis' moustache. In part this is due to the limitations of photography, at that time, to correctly portray some kinds of shining coloured hair.

The hair on Louis' head and especially his moustache was not of a thick and course variety, lacking reflection. Each hair in his case was thin and fine, with a translucence due to transparency and refraction which showed to the naked eye as having an attractive golden or copper sheen, but which was an impossible colour for photography to portray and as a result his hair in images often appears to be jet black.

It must be borne in mind that I am not in the least blaming the photographers for their failure, in not giving Louis his light bright hair. Perhaps a noted and skilful photographer could have avoided such drab and dreary untrue results seen in most of Louis' photographs. I do possess one photograph in which the light and bright hair of another sitter, not Louis, is beautifully depicted and which otherwise would have been black on a print.

All the photos of Louis that I have given a dismal and depressive appearance of him in my view, whereas he was anything but! He was ever bright, like his hair, and his eyes shone forth with the gaiety of his soul. Everyone who knew Louis will remember that his moustache was thin and so pale in colour that it formed nearly an unnoticeable feature on his face. Yet in almost every photograph, Louis' moustache appears to be a marked facial feature! The small touch of hair below Louis lower lip was also barely noticeable for the same reason. Louis' moustache was not only very delicate but was also flat with his face and in no way bushy. But these errors in darkness added another feature in all his photos. That was the tendency to make Louis' face look pale by contrast. Louis, while not ruddy in the face, was not pallid or pasty looking. Indeed, he looked jolly fine and bright.

It is true Louis had no pink blush on his cheek nor had a clear translucent appearance and complexion, yet all was in harmony. The opinion expressed by the medical profession and repeated up until his death, was that there was no reason he should not live 'till he was 80 years old.' But I come now to attempt to correct impressions many seem to have, and it is important, as not even one of his photos, of which there are so many in number, reveals much of Louis' mentality. They are not 'Louis'!! They are of a 'being' sitting to have its photograph taken! I use the word 'its' advisedly.

Although many may say that Louis enjoyed having his photograph taken, in my view his photographs, pictures and sculptures, did not capture the real 'Louis', who was ever gay and bright. How incredibly sad this is.

He had a continuous laugh upon his lips, surely an unquestionable advantage for anyone to have. He had an enthralling smile that seemed not only to illuminate his face but to radiate from his soul and eyes, not only when he was speaking or when others were addressing him, but at all reasonable times.

The idea that one had to be solemn as well as steady was not in any way an obsession on his part. At that time and particularly in Louis' younger days, it was by necessity strongly forced upon the sitter to remain absolutely still, before the introduction of rapid film photography. The requirement to be solemn to maintain steadiness had been understood by Louis, but unfortunately had stayed with him throughout his life when it came to photography.

Even in his later life whether he was posing for the photographer, painter or sculptor, the artists' failed to grasp the outstanding tell-tale of Louis' life which radiated from his eyes and face; that they had a happy and interested 'being' before them.

These men of undoubted ability and talent somehow failed to capture Louis' soul and the mentality before them. They only portrayed a man in a pose, ready to have his portrait taken.

Portrait by John Singer Sargent.

John Singer Sargent's fine painting of Louis depicted a particular pose and mood but even here it is not a portrait showing Louis' personality as being ever gay and bright. Sargent portrays him in a state of careful consideration, perhaps contemplating a romance, or how best to run his next plot. Judging from Louis' appearance of seeming deep in thought, which is admirably depicted, indeed the tale might be on the eve of completion. However, I can accept that Sargent painted an undoubted likeness of 'Louis' from the crown of his head to the tip of his little finger – yes – a King of Romance.

Louis' Enjoyment of Life

Louis did not share in the usual fun of boys with games such as football, golf, cricket or the rigging and sailing of model yachts. None of these appealed to Louis, he was not smitten by a single one of them. As for fencing, the horizontal gym bar or boxing, the very name of such was too much for Louis! He did not play 'hails', a game with 'clacken' bat and ball that the Edinburgh Academy boys played daily at every moment they were free from their masters' domination. Louis did not like the game so his days at the Academy, and I don't wonder, were hateful to him and he thus missed the best part of the fun – indeed the whole part of where fun could be found at school – as he absented often. Reading and writing were his outstanding pleasures.

Whenever I met Louis in his young days, he was always bright and never seemed unhappy or ill. Louis had his own pleasures, such as riding, canoeing – and so can anyone believe Louis did not enjoy life as much as his neighbours, seeing he got what he desired most, vis-a-vis reading and 'writing'. Look again at the huge amount that he wrote beginning with his history of Moses and on from that until the hour of his death, when he was engaged on *The Weir of Hermiston*. During all his life, one may say, he was working, nay working hard, at the main pleasure of his life, which was 'writing'.

Further, does anyone believe that Louis didn't enjoy himself ... at Mentone, in Paris, Grez, at Swanton, on his six month trip to Naples with my sister Bessy, during the times at our house at 25 Royal Terrace, at 45 Melville Street, watching the theatricals at Great Stuart Street, spending time with his donkey, rowing in his canoes, spent at San Francisco, during the times with cousin Bob – that adorable man and then finishing with not only a yacht, the *Casco,* but actually taking a voyage on her in his beloved Pacific, the choice of his life to do so. The list of activities and events is endless. Those who knew Louis were aware throughout his life that he was doing absolutely and entirely the very thing he was most keen to do. None should believe for an instant that

Louis had a life of incessant want for strength and pleasure, as some seem to think, on account of his repeated illnesses. Yet those that there were, didn't prevent him from pursuing his great pleasure of writing.

Even to his last moments Louis was writing and he had the satisfaction of knowing that his great work *The Weir of Hermiston* was on the eve of completion. The impression of a drab, dingy and dull existence in which illnesses have been portrayed as the main feature of Louis' life must pale before the joyous fact that this was not so. On the contrary, Louis had plenty of health and strength to enjoy his time and was not confined to being seen as an invalid throughout his life. To his very last days he rode on horseback dressed all 'booted and spurred' (but actually without spurs) as was his usual custom.

Until Louis went to Samoa he had always expected to die and be buried in Scotland, be it either in the 'gated cell' where his father laid, or somewhere on the Pentlands. Even when he had reached Samoa he still hoped to die in his native Scotland. However, it was not to be.

On the left is a somewhat imperfect photograph,
however its informality reveals RLS in a natural pose.
On the right is an engraving of RLS, created by Charles himself.

Thoughts of Childhood in Verse

Louis dedicated his major work of children's poetry to Cummie,
who had looked after him through thick and thin, during his childhood.

From the beginning to the end, I have tried to select the content among Louis' work that seemed the best for young children by following the practice adopted in many of our nursery rhymes, namely brevity and having few verses. Thus, these should be suitable for young children and much the better for retaining in the memory, of both young and old.

Bed in Summer

In winter I sit up at night
And dress by yellow candle-light
In summer, quite the other way
I have to go to bed by day.

And does it not seem hard to you,
When all the sky is clear and blue,
And I should like so much to play,
To have to go to bed by day?

A Thought

It is very nice to think
The world is full of meat and drink,
The little children saying grace
In every Christian kind of place.

Whole Duty of Children

A child should always say what's true,
And speak when he is spoken to,
And behave mannerly at table:
At least as far as he is able.

Foreign Lands

Of speckled eggs the birdie sings
And nests among the trees:
The sailor sings of ropes and things
In ships upon the sea.

Where Do My Boats Go

Dark brown is the river,
Golden is the sand
It flows along for ever
With trees on either hand.

Green leaves a-floating,
Castles of the foam,
Boats of mine a-boating –
Where will all come home?

On goes the river
And out past the mill
Away down the valley,
Away down the hill.

Away down the river
A hundred miles or more,
Other little children
Shall bring my boats ashore.

The Land of Nod

From breakfast on all through the day
At home among my friends I stay;
But every night I go abroad
Afar into the land of Nod.

My Orange

Every night my prayers I say,
And get my dinner every day:
And every day that I've been good
I get an orange after food.

A Good Boy

I woke before the morning but I was happy all the day,
I never said an ugly word but smiled and stuck to play.

And now at last the sun is going down behind the wood,
And I am happy, for I know that I've been good.

My bed is waiting cool and fresh, with linen smooth and fair,
And I must off to sleepsin-by and not forget my prayer.

The Moon

The moon has a face like the clock in the hall;
She shines on thieves on the garden wall,
On streets and fields and harbour quays,
And birdies asleep in the forks of the trees.

The Swing

How do you like to go up in a swing,
Up in the air so blue?
Oh, I do think it the pleasantest thing
Ever a child can do!

Up in the air and over the wall,
Till I can see so wide,
Rivers and trees and cattle and all
Over the countryside –

Till I look down on the garden green,
Down on the roof so brown –
Up in the air I go flying again,
Up in the air and down!

Time to Rise

A birdie with a yellow bill
Hopped upon the windowsill,
Cocked his shining eye and said
Ain't you 'shamed, you sleepy-head!

In Bed

Then, when mamma goes by the bed,
She shall come in with tip-toe tread,
And see me lying warm and fast
And in the Land of Nod at last.

At the Seaside

When I went down beside the sea,
A wooden spade they gave to me
To dig the sandy shore.
My holes were empty like a cup,
In every hole the sea came up,
Till it could come no more.

The style Louis favoured to adopt throughout his series of nursery rhymes, that of giving the child's version of what he or she thought, is illustrated in the first of his verses 'Bed in Summer' where the child describes their own feelings.

There is no doubt to me that Louis struck the right note in giving the child's version. His series of verses show the wonderful facility he had of capturing the thoughts of children. He put these thoughts down in a language that I feel few can criticise.

The approach of Louis was not altogether unknown in earlier times. As an example, the well-known nursery rhyme giving the child's own view being 'Twinkle, twinkle little star….'.

As an aside, I recited this famous rhyme at a school exhibition with my mother (Louis' devoted Aunt Elizabeth) seated at my side, her gentle but firm hand emboldening me – a mere wee mite – through a nerve-racking ordeal.

Finally, a poem that seems the perfect bedtime story:

The Lamplighter

My tea is nearly ready and the sun has left the sky;
It's time to take the window to see Leerie going by;
For every night at tea-time and before you take your seat,
With lantern and with ladder he comes posting up the street.

Now Tom would be the driver and Maria go to sea;
And my papa's a banker and as rich as he can be;
But I, when I am stronger and can choose what I'm to do,
O Leerie, I'll go round at night and light the lamps with you!

For we are very lucky, with a lamp before the door,
And Leerie stops to light it as he lights so many more;
And O! Before you hurry by the ladder and with light,
Oh Leerie, see a little child and nod to him to-night!

Louis' Dog Coolin

A handful of years of Louis' life had scarcely flown by when there was another addition to the family in the shape of a dog named Coolin. This dog must have been something of a power in helping to round off rough corners of discord within the family, as all three – father, mother and child – loved Coolin. The inclusion of such a small thing into a household can bring wonders.

Coolin was a Skye terrier, named fittingly after that range of hills on Skye, with their serrated peaks of great grandeur. The name of the hills in Gaelic being nearly unspellable (An Cuithionn) and pronounced vulgarly, 'The Coolins'. Louis had his little grey-haired friend with him for about 12 years. Coolin was buried in the garden of his parents' house at Swanston, near Edinburgh.

The photograph below was taken by my father, David Stevenson, when Coolin was about 8 years old. Louis' father, Thomas, was present when the photograph was taken, as was I. I kept the positive in my possession.

*It is a shame that this photograph from more than
150 years ago is now in such poor condition.*

Thomas Stevenson – The Boy's Father

Thomas perhaps was the least driven of Robert Stevenson's sons and it seems may have been more like Robert Louis Stevenson, his own son, than many realised. Robert Stevenson, the famous engineer, was very patient with young Thomas, as he could see that the two elder sons were settled well into engineering. However, Thomas was free to choose his own career. He seemed destined to write visionary stories, visit all the antique bookshops Edinburgh had to offer and study natural science. Finally, he was noted for sleeping in, as long as he liked in the morning.

A story told to me by my father David, described an incident he remembered from their home at Baxter Place when he and Tom were still children. Tom was reported to be 'lying in bed and wouldn't get up'. So, brother Bob, who later became a surgeon in the army, was told to examine him and as usual found it was a case of shamming illness to escape classes at school. On completion of his examination Bob left the room and returned, furnished with a pickled gherkin which he pushed up one of Tom's nostrils and then he left the room. 'The result was immediate success!'

After leaving school, Thomas tried many directions for his early career, including book printing, book selling and publishing. Eventually boredom drove him to ask his father for an apprenticeship in the family firm. This meant enrolling at Edinburgh University, together with work experience in the office and site work during his holidays. There followed continuous advice from Robert on the need for early rising and a letter from his father ending with the words, 'Set your mind and your shoulders to the world and press on.' Indeed, by the age of 21 years, Thomas was a changed man and was hard at work in the firm designing surveying instruments and supervising the erection of his first lighthouse.

From then on, he forsook his earlier lazy ways, indeed he worked extremely hard. His devout belief in Christianity, inherited from the previous generation, was a strength he could always call upon. Hence it must have been a terrible shock when, in 1873, Louis declared that he was no longer a Christian. However perhaps that could have been predicted, as Thomas' own views on children's education were light-years away from those of his contemporaries. He believed that children only learnt what they wanted to learn and at the time when they were ready.

It should be understood that Thomas and Louis shared a talent that was really a love of words, and they were great sparing partners both in public and private. Louis writes of his father:

His talk compounded of so much sterling sense and so much freakish humour and clothed in language so apt, droll and emphatic, was a perpetual delight to all who knew him... His affections and emotions were liable to passionate ups and downs, found the most eloquent expressions both in words and gestures. Love, anger and indignation shone through him and broke forth in imagery.

In conclusion, Louis recognised in his father the depressive state that was mutual to them both.

Louis In Prison – The Snowball Riot

While attending Edinburgh University, Louis had a curious experience into which his father got dragged. There was a snowball fight, or riot, at the principal gate, between the students and the public. Louis was not involved. He was watching the riotous activity from outside the university building when the police arrived and marched off the students, including Louis, all being taken to the police station. A friend of Louis went down Heriot Row to see Thomas in order to request bail for Louis and ask him to be released from custody. The response from Louis' father was, 'No member of the Stevenson family has ever been to jail before, and Louis must just suffer the penalty.'

Louis' friend objected by saying, 'Then I remain here in your house.' Ultimately Thomas gave in, handed over the money and Louis was let out of jail that night. All went well the next day in court; 'No detention for the snowballers.'

Louis' Literary Work Devoid of Boasting

It is a feature of Louis' work, that he made no boast of his ancestors, the lasting nature of their achievements or their Christian strength. He avoided any temptation to brag of the family's reputation. It might be thought that Louis didn't fully appreciate the great difficulty and accomplishment of his grandfather's work in building the Bell Rock Lighthouse. Instead, he would refer to the fact that a child might play on the rock gathering pebbles and shells scooping salt water with pail from one pool or another. Louis did not point out the fact that on the very spot at low water where the child might be playing would in two hours' time have five feet of water over it and in six hours this would indeed be 15 feet underwater.

But Louis was romancing with a strong 'author's licence'. Perhaps Louis, even more forcibly underplaying the achievements of his ancestral forebears, dubbed his great-grandfather Smith as 'the lamp and oil man'. This seems unfair. Smith was never so simple. He was an optical genius with his oils, his lamps and his reflectors – making huge strides in solving the problems of optical efficiency. Smith was a multi-faceted man; being a ship-owner, a born architect, as well as being a skilled engineer.

Skye

Sing me a song of a lad that is gone
Say could that lad be I?
Merry of soul he sailed on a day
Over the sea to Skye.

Mull was astern, Rum on the port
Eigg on the starboard bow
Glory of youth glowed in his soul
Where is the glory now?

Sing me a song of a lad that is gone
Say could that lad be I?
Merry of soul he sailed on the day
Over the sea to Skye.

Louis' track to Skye is shown in my sketch below. Skerryvore and Dhu Heartach lighthouses are shown towards the bottom.

Iona and Dhu Heartach

The chart shows a part of Scotland well known to Louis. It shows where the brig *Covenant*, described by Louis in his novel *Kidnapped*, was wrecked upon the Torrin Rocks on the south side of the island of Mull. The vessel sank and the crew, 'saved themselves as best they could'. One of Louis' heroes David Balfour, being cast on the Isle of Erraid. This island is marked as Dorri, on the right edge of the chart and note the area dotted that the island is joined to the shore of Mull by a beach which covers over at high tide. David Balfour used this beach to cross and make his way across Mull and on to the mainland of Scotland.

Louis was on the island of Erraid for two or three weeks to learn the profession of civil engineering, while the Dhu Heartach Lighthouse was being built. I was at Erraid and at Dhu Heartach before work on the lighthouses began. The Dhu Heartach lighthouse was designed by my father, David Stevenson. I was there as the tower was being built and visited again several times after it was completed. The lighthouse is on the outermost of that group of rocks (or hotter as sailors call such a group) named the Torrin Rocks. The Skerryvore Lighthouse built by Louis' uncle Alan Stevenson is also nearby.

Sam Bough an eminent painter was commissioned by my father, to paint a picture of the Dhu Heartach Lighthouse while it was being built. This painting is in the possession of my son D. Alan Stevenson. At the time of Sam Bough's visit, the light had particularly brilliance, as is evident in his painting. Even more brilliant was the water, with its combination of shallow reflection from the white sand beneath, the heavy surf on the rock itself gleaming white in sharp contrast with Sam Bough's blue of the ocean.

Alan and the Stevenson Gaiety of Spirit

Alan Stevenson was uncle to both Louis and me. His poetical powers were not confined to the more serious side of life but extended into verse to amuse his own children, Louis and our family. Here are some lines to exemplify the grand fun which permeated Alan's whole life.

One from Edinburgh:

There was a man whose name was Scott
Who was a priest and yet was not

One from Glasgow:

Breakfast was over at Carleton Place
Old Lawrie rubbed his nose
And thus unto his wife he spoke
In accents most jocose

One from North Berwick:

Then long life to our noble King
And Strathie long live he
And when he next doth round the Bass
May I be there to see.

However, Alan Stevenson's engineering triumph was undoubtedly designing and erecting the Skerryvore Lighthouse.

Louis thus described the lighthouse:

Eternal granite hewn from the living isle* and dowelled with brute iron, rears the tower.**

That, from its wet foundation to its crown of glittering glass***, stands in the sweep of winds, immovable, immortal, eminent. ****

* From Tiree on the west coast of Scotland.
** Alan Stevenson designed and 'reared the tower'.
*** Its illuminated crown was the most powerful light in the world.
**** 158 feet high and remains to this day 'eminent' and unchallenged.
Lit in 1844.

Alan made the curve of the tower a hyperbola. Louis is wrong when he says that Skerryvore was 'dowelled with brute iron'. Alan Stevenson designed the stones to be tree-nailed following in the footsteps of Seaton at Eddystone and Robert Stevenson at Bell Rock. My father improved on this by using stone ribband and stone joggling in his Dhu Heartach and Chicken Rock towers. At Skerryvore the treenails were of oak and greenheart but there was no iron. The rock is hard gneiss intersected by numerous gullies and the surface has more the appearance of dark-coloured glass than a reef of Gneiss-rock. The whole surface even in the gullies had a submarine cavern that threw up a jet of water sometimes 20 feet in height – with a loud noise like the snorting of some sea monster. The cavern terminated in a polished spherical chamber, beautifully smooth and glassy. The cavity was filled up for safety in the building process and to save the men working there from being drenched with the spray.

Landing on the polished rock was a very hazardous business especially at the commencement of work and there were many accidents caused by the slipperiness of the surface.

*Illustration of the completed Skerryvore Lighthouse
contained in David Stevenson's book of its building and the
then unique light system designed by Alan, which was adopted.*

Louis' love for the best of this world's pleasures – a happy home – was not confined to his uncle David and aunt Elizabeth's household, as he had an open door also to his uncle Alan and aunt Margaret's house at Portobello, with their three lovely and attractive daughters and their adorable son, Bob. Alan, like his brother David, was beloved by all who were lucky enough to know him. Neither of them was considered to be tyrannical bigots and they both welcomed the views of others with generous and kindly feelings.

Alan was highly skilled in engineering and mathematics as well as having literary tastes in no small order. His optical improvements at the Isle of

May, at Skerryvore and at North Ronaldsay made them outshine all other lights. It was he who made our lights 'shine more brightly'.

His wife, my aunt Margaret, was indeed a star in her own right. She was comely and graced with nature's beauty as well as having charming manners that no one could fail to notice and appreciate; a skill she handed down to each of her three daughters.

Alan and Margaret's only son Bob (Robert Alan Mowbray Stevenson) was a most lovely youth, ever cheery and bright, with the same gracious manner as the rest of the family. He was for a time professor of Fine Art in Liverpool. He made his mark both as a painter and as an author, both of which led to him cementing a bond of friendship between himself and Louis that continued throughout their lives.

Muckle Flugga and North Unst

As with other family forebears, Louis did not boast of his Uncle David's work. David was for more than 40 years Engineer to the Commissioners of Northern Lighthouses and did one of the boldest pieces of lighthouse engineering that was ever accomplished, this being at Muckle Flugga in the Shetland Isles.

The difficulties that David had to overcome in this unique engineering work were great indeed. From David's own notes this extract gives some flavour of the problems:

I sailed for Shetland on 17th February 1854. The weather was wretched, and the passage was most uncomfortable and upon arriving at Lerwick on Saturday night at 11 o'clock, having experienced considerable difficulty in finding the entrance to the Bay, we were informed that the last mail received at Shetland from the mainland was on 1st December (the previous year) and that the winter had been an unusually severe one. There were no steamers trading there at that time and the poor Shetlanders who had been nearly three months without communication received our printed and verbal news with great interest... Our appearance off the coast at that season of the year caused no small speculation among the simple island folk. Rumours of war with the Russians it seems had reached them... They all retreated to the interior leaving their houses to our mercy. We learned afterwards that they were afraid either of the press gang or that we might indeed be Russians.

With reference to the work of erecting the temporary lighthouse I would mention that the weight of materials to be landed at the rock was 120 tons which sometimes had to be hauled through the surf and then everything had to be carried 200 feet up the rock, on the backs of men, there being no time to prepare any other appliance. The whole of this first structure was laden, taken up and David (my father) and Thomas (Louis' father) worked together

37

to design and build the lighthouse and the shore station on North Unst. To me this is a most interesting location. built in just 26 days, being on an outlying rock – the most northerly habitable spot in the British Isles.

The permanent lighthouse of Muckle Flugga on North Unst was completed two years later.

Out Stack is the most northerly point of the British Isles just a little rock at latitude 60 degrees 52'. This point is visible from the North Unst Lighthouse. At the longest day the sun is but a short time below the horizon. A little further north and one is in the region of the midnight sun. Out Stack has been described as 'The fill stop at the end of Britain'. Travellers heading due north would not encounter any further land mass between here and the North Pole. John Franklin's widow landed here on her way searching for her husband in his pursuit of the Northwest Passage.

This photograph of Out Stack was taken from the lighthouse.

Before the physicist Marconi came to this country from Italy, I had suggested that the communication between the lighthouse and the shore station should be by wireless. Electric transmitters and receivers would be installed in both locations. The design and a full description are recorded in the transactions of the Royal Society of Edinburgh.

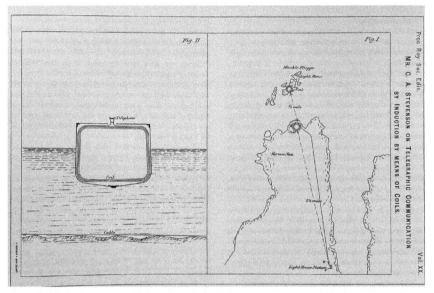

The North Unst Lighthouse was built in 1854, with its purpose originally declared as being to protect shipping for the Crimea War, surprising but shipping was reliant on the prevailing winds. North Unst was visited by Louis and the islet became his inspiration for the map of 'Treasure Island'.

Louis' Playground

The country over which I will describe as being Louis' playground in East Lothian, consists mainly of agricultural land. The landscape owes its configuration to the action of ice-flow. The surface has at one time been worn away by glacial movement coming from the direction of Edinburgh, grinding and scraping away the softer material leaving the harder rocks sticking up with precipices on their eastern or sheltered sides. The surfaces of the rocks to this day in many places as shown by the arrows on my later map, retain the glacier's scouring action in the form of scratches and grooves. It is interesting how the very small scratches are still visible, notwithstanding weathering, although many years have passed. Compare the glacier action in Switzerland with the visible scratches on our rock surfaces and then decide if you think it can have been so very long ago since all this country was ice bound. The hard rocks have been left sticking up like monuments in the landscape owing to their greater hardness, examples being North Berwick Law, the Garleton Hills with its Hopetoun monument, Traprain Law and the four islets opposite north Berwick all worn on the southwestern sides by the ice. These hills and islets were all well known to Louis. The islets form a very marked and unusual feature in the landscape and are described in some of his novels.

The Pavilion on the Links

Louis' *The Pavilion on the Links* is based on the actual place where he and I played together as boys. It is on the shore opposite to the Isle of Fidra, close to North Berwick and at the north end of a wood that reached down from Archerfield House to the sea.

I remember how keen Louis was on noting whether the pavilion there happened to be shuttered or not. It tended to vary and this variation, while of no interest to me, evidently was meaningful to Louis for his tale. Furthermore, any event such as people walking alone on the broad sands would be noted by him. In those days there were few people about. So very different to the present day. The bents were an ideal hiding place for supposed smugglers and robbers, with their undulation of hillocks and hollows and the natural bunkers of sand. The whole of Archerfield with its links, woods and bents, sands and islets and sea vista are redolent, if one may use such a term, of Louis' marvellous tale of *The Pavilion on the Links*.

Frank Cassilis, the narrator, recounts how while at college a friend named Northmour had once invited him to his pavilion home at Graden-Easter, a wild place with stretches of sand-hills, links and windswept scrub by the coast. After a violent argument, however, the two had parted and had not spoken for nine years.

Cassilis now returns to Graden-Easter on his wandering travels, almost as a gypsy. Unobserved, he sees a bent old man, a young woman and Northmour land on the beach from a boat at night, then make their way stealthily into the pavilion under cover of darkness. When Cassilis steps forward to address Northmour, the latter attacks him for no apparent reason, wounding him slightly with a knife. While not seriously harmed and being still curious about Northmour's actions, Cassilis decides to keep watch on the house.

He often sees the young woman, Clara Huddlestone, walking on the beach. During these walks she is pursued by Northmour, whose attentions to her are rejected. When Clara nearly steps into a quicksand, Cassilis saves her. She then tells him that her father had been a private banker. When her father's affairs became disordered, he tried 'dangerous and at last, criminal expedients to retrieve himself from ruin'. This included involvement with the Italian Carbonari, members of a secret political association. The Italians were now pursuing him for the money he had lost. Northmour had pledged to help them out of their trouble, hiding them in the deserted pavilion, on condition that the old man Mr Huddlestone would give Clara to him in marriage.

Cassilis decides to investigate the story. While reading about the Huddlestone case in the newspapers, he is startled to see three Italians in the village. When he returns to the pavilion, he detects footsteps leading to the quicksand and the hat of one of the Italians – who had been at the house and on the way, one had sunk to his death.

Cassilis vows to protect Clara from the Italian threat and despite the rivalry between Northmour and Cassilis over Clara, Northmour accepts the help, displaying the duality of his character. The Italians surround the house, then set it on fire. The four inside look to flee. Old man Huddlestone pushes the others aside and leads the way out, in an act of surrender. The Italians shoot Huddlestone dead.

The story ends with Northmour taunting Cassilis over who is the more honourable towards Clara – a balance of valour – love getting the better of lust. Northmour again demonstrates the duality of his personality, concedes and sails off, leaving Clara and Cassilis to marry.

Dirleton Quicksand

The sands below Dirleton had an unenviable reputation. There was a story attached to them of the swallowing up of a man, a cart and horse in quicksand. Louis' exploration down to the low water mark proved of no avail in finding anything other than a softness which one may find on many a beach due to entrapped seaweed.

Louis, nothing daunted, threw all examination and doubts to the winds with his love for romance and daring in *Pavilion on the Links.* He accepted as authentic the old legend of the quicksand. In his story he knew the exact location of the danger in the quicksand and stopped his heroine from walking straight to her death.

Louis made double use of the quicksand as in his tale, he sent one of his enemies to his death there. The gulls evidently had seen the ruffian being engulfed by the quicksand and wheeled over his sepulchre with their triumphant and melancholy piping.

It was a clever thought of Louis to have gulls actually circling above the deadly spot and this in a chaste manner signalling the site. Louis, in his many walks along the beach, never let slip an opportunity from real life. Hence with a grave face he would impress on others the advisability of keeping well up to the dry sand when walking along the beach. The hulls of full masted vessels have been known to disappear 'holus bolus' in our estuary. Then why not have a Dirleton quicksand. Evidently suction!

An incident occurred here on one occasion when I was with Louis. With my walking stick I had flicked a bone from a stranded sheep's jaw, which flew up hitting Louis in the face. No serious damage was done but he gave me a well-deserved 'round of the guns'. It was an ever-recurrent piece of fun among us boys to flick with one's stick a piece of driftwood or tangle of weed or sand – but a bone! No.

The one other occasion when I got into his bad books was on the banks of the Forth at Stirling. He and I had been examining a beech tree on which my father, years before, had cut his initials DS and those of his beloved one. I very stupidly picked out the centre of the letter D with a knife. Louis in his horror saw that piece of bark was gone – such a heinous sin in Louis' eyes. I received a well-deserved dressing down from him.

To the east of these fateful Dirleton sands, still a terror to many who know the legend of the missing horse and cart saga, lies Longskelly Beach – known now as the Broad Sands.

My photograph shows a heavy sea with the waves breaking on the beach. At the distant end of the beach are the wreaths of sand, forming the sand hills with North Berwick Law in the far distance.

North Berwick and the Islets

The map shows Alan Breck and David's track from Edinburgh to the Broad Sands below Dirleton and then David's track behind North Berwick Law to Tantallon Castle and across the Firth of Forth to the Bass Rock. The map also shows with arrows, the direction of the ice scratches on the rock surfaces that still exist, which I referred to earlier. The general direction of the ice flow which sculpted Louis' playground is said to be from the West to East.

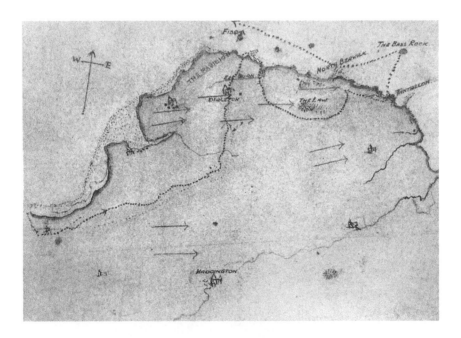

Ibris, Fidra, the Lamb, Craigleith and the Bass lie almost in a straight line off the coast of North Berwick as shown on the map. Ibris, which is the furthest west, rises to only a few feet in height above high-water level. Duck eggs used to be gathered in abundance on this rock at the right season. The duck egg is perhaps the finest of all seabird eggs being not only large in size but of exceptionally delicate flavour.

The Lamb is basaltic like the rest of these islets. The needle of a mariner's compass erected on the top of this islet is much deflected from magnetic north by the magnetic power of the islet itself. A hand specimen broken from the rock, when held near a compass needle will deflect the needle by many degrees just like a piece of ladestone.

Craigleith, like its neighbours, has a precipitous face on its eastern side showing how this surface must have been saved from the direct flow of the ice which passed from west to east.

Fidra is the furthest west of a group of three Islets, excluding the small rock of Ibris. The island of Fidra was well described by Louis as being:

> *a strange grey islet of two humps, made more conspicuous by a piece of ruin and I mind that, as we draw close to it. The sea peeped through like a man's eye.*

The eye hole through the main hump is about 30 feet in height. In Louis' day the eye used to be very marked, being a lovely feature of Fidra. Seen from as far away as the road leading out of Dirleton towards North Berwick, the eye, with the sea behind, looked like a waterfall.

However, in recent years trees have grown up so high as to shut off this unique appearance of a great waterfall pouring out of the island itself. Tarbet is the name of the smaller of the two humps mentioned by Louis, which is formed by the basaltic rock common in Scotland and signifies a narrow neck of little height separating the sea on each side.

As a footnote the Lighthouse built on Fidra was a joint project by David (Charles' father) and Thomas (Louis' father) in 1885 and what is described above, predates its building.

The Bass Rock
The Bass Rock is the most easterly of the islets and is by far the most interesting. The top of the rock is shaven off by the ice flow, to the west and south. The rock itself is otherwise precipitous even to overhang in places.

Bass Rock: Engraving of 1870. It should be noted the prison building is there but no lighthouse until 1903.

Bass Rock at one time was used as a state prison, the ruins of which remain to this day. The Bass is a somewhat weird protrusion from the sea, as one realises on effecting a landing and clambering over its steep and oft slippery slopes. It has an 'eye' like its neighbour Fidra. The eye at the Bass does not show daylight right through as the hole has a bend on it. The eye runs roughly east to west and is 30 feet in height and is about 170 yards in length.

There are other 'eyes' along the coast to the south of the Bass such as at Dunbar and Coldingham. There is also one on the cliffs a few miles north of Berwick-on-Tweed.

The sea birds which are very numerous had occasionally deserted the top of the rock during Charles' time.

Bass is described by Louis in *Catriona* as an 'unco place', meaning that it is an exceptionally weird place and that its inhabitants, including the solan goose (also known as the northern gannet), can also seem weird.

Here is Louis' tale of the taking of young solan geese, shorn I fear of its beauty, by not putting Louis' fine touch to the description and from the fact that the tale is a translation from the Scots tongue that is so full of words that sound like what they mean. Indeed, the full meaning is perhaps a little lost in my translation. Forgive me.

It was the season of the year to take young solans, which were captured by the cragsman, who was aided by and sometimes completely and entirely suspended by a rope held near the top of a cliff and manoeuvred by four strong and capable lads. Many a time one of these cragsmen would relate his experience and always the sweat ran down him when he told his thrilling tale.

Tam, the cragsman, was hanging from the precipice with the solans skirling and flying around him. It chanced that Tam glanced up and saw a large solan pecking at the rope, 'Shoo,' said Tam, 'Away with you.'

The solan peered down into Tam's face and there was something weird in the creature's glance. Just one glance it gave, then back to the rope but now the bird wrought and wrenched at it as if mad. The bird seemed to understand its work well, as it was bruising the rope against a sharp edge of the rock. Tam had a cold fit of fear in his heart. 'This thing is no more bird', thought he and he signalled for the lads to pull him up. The solan seemed to understand about the signal for no sooner had the signal been made that the solan let go of the rope, spread its wings, screeched out. It took a single turn flying and dashed straight at Tam's eyes – Tam took out his knife and the solan seemed to understand about knives as soon as it saw the blade gleamed in the sun. The solan gave one squawk of seeming disappointment and flew off round the Rock and Tam saw him no more. The men pulled Tam up like a dead corpse bumping against the rock as he was drawn up. Some brandy soon revived Tam.

That there is no exaggeration about this tale and that Tam was unhinged may be judged from my own experience when I was alone on the face of a cliff on the Island of Lewis. A bird overhead had seen that in a few seconds I would have scrambled over to reach its nest of eggs on the cliff face. The first I knew of anything being wrong was seeing and hearing a thing of many square feet hurtling straight at me. The whole saga took place in just a few seconds.

The presence of something else on the cliff face besides me; the noise of the rush of air as the bird passed a foot above my head; the darkening of the sky as the bird passed. In a few moments all was over and I found myself at the nest with its eggs! I must admit I was a bit unnerved with the sight of the sea hundreds of feet below. The bird's attack on Tam was much more severe than in my case and it is no wonder that he was entirely unhinged by the time he was pulled up to safety.

It is very interesting to see solan geese diving for fish from 100 feet and more above the sea, falling as they do like a stone, sending up a small splash of water and remaining down for a long time, sometimes for as much as two minutes and then surfacing with their fishy catch and flying off to the rock to feed their young. Solan geese lay but one egg per season. The egg of a solan is large and nearly white.

With a dark sky east of Bass and with the sun shining on the rock itself, it is a wondrous sight; the stark white of the birds like a cloud against the black background of the rock. The lovely effect is perhaps best seen at sunset from North Berwick.

Indeed, bird life was subject of daily interest to Louis. He knew the strength of the solan goose and its intelligence. He loved the call of the curlew and the song of our garden birds, the caw of the crow and the screech of the seagull, with its key-aw, key-aw, key-aw.

Louis greatly advanced the public's knowledge of Bass by adding it in his novel *Catriona*. That inimitable tale including Bass in which he encouraged interest, that good and true North Berwickers naturally had for Bass Rock. It is such a majestic sight at their very door. Furthermore, Louis successfully linked the subtle ethereal chain of a superhuman order to Bass Rock with events in the minds of the inhabitants ashore. Many, upon reading Louis' tale, would find that it made their very innards feel 'funny', as it is so eerily told.

There seem to be no words in English to fully express the feeling involved or to match with the Scots words – 'weird', 'superstitious' or 'eerie', that are applicable to Bass, because these words include or involve a superhuman agency far beyond the English words awe, dread, fear, ghostly or even haunted. Louise loved the Scottish tongue and deplored its gradual decline.

Damming the Eel Burn

A source of amusement for us boys was the damming of the Eel Burn. This burn which Louis referred to in *Catriona* as a 'cressy burn', was a mile west of the North Berwick Links.

It was an ideal place for a dam with plenty of water from a large drainage area round about Dirleton and with an abundance of sand and no rocks or stone. There was no one to disturb us in those days; a joyous lot for boys, with no illness I can assure you!

After the dam's completion, what a cataract to look forward to, upon its bursting! Niagara is as nothing compared to our cataract as we ourselves will make – reminding one of the Glasgow skipper's rejoinders, 'God made your Mississippi no doubt but we Glasgow and Greenock folk made the Clyde.'

A permanent diversion of the burn was the vain idea of our youthful minds. In our heads was the thought that we could make such a change. But 'lack a day' and a high tide with an onshore wind, our efforts were entirely dashed in a single night so that not a vestige was left.

There were many other attractions which boys were engaged upon at North Berwick in Louis' young days such as building rafts, sailing model boats, riding ponies, home-made bicycles, clecking for partans (waiting for crabs to hatch) and so on. But now all these amusements are gone and golf reigns supreme in house and home, on what was then our playground. How times do change.

Back then, North Berwick had an abundance of interests to pursue. Louis said of golf that he had something better to do than play that game. Louis, to a large extent, ignored many of the other boys' amusements and instead he took forward a very keen interest to role play as robbers and villains. We had many happy times in the bents between North Berwick and Durleton Links playing at such on the very self-same ground that figured so largely in his wonderful works *Catriona* and *The Pavilion on the Links*.

The Black Rock

The Black Rock photographed by CAS.

As a child, Louis often played on the Black Rock, shown in my photograph above. The Black Rock lies near the high-water mark at the far end of the East Bay of North Berwick. The rock has been for many years, the scene of nursery maids sewing, knitting and chatting as well as being the meeting place for children, of which Louis was one, playing around, armed with wooden spade and pail. I loved the rock. Although the rock seems inaccessible for young children, I am sure the mere memory of the rock is treasured by thousands. The fact that the rock may be difficult to climb adds interest to its beauty just as the difficulty of ascending the Matterhorn undoubtedly adds to the majestic glory and beauty of that mountain.

Charles and David Stevenson, dressed up as
many young boys were at that time.

Boating

The home-made 'land' boat made by me and my brother when we were small children, shown in the photograph below, was particularly successful.

Charles and his elder brother David 'boating' at Anchor House.

The hull was made out of tea chests, the mast was a clothes-drying pole. As for the rest – two toy guns on deck, thole pins, sails, bladders and anchor (a stone one) – the materials were collected from the beach. The boat is being steered by me and as described in Louis's words, 'I am a-steering of the boat.'

Louis must have been charmed with this boat; I am sure all was A1 in his mind! The photograph taken by my father is a little later than Louis described in his verse below.

A-Sailing on the Billows

We built a ship upon the stairs
All made of back-bedroom chairs
And filled it full of sofa pillows.

We took a saw and several nails and water in the nursery pails:

And Tom said 'Let us also take
An apple and a slice of cake.'
Which was enough for Tom and me
To go a-sailing on till tea.

We sailed along for days and days,
And had the very best of plays.
But Tom fell out and hurt his knee,
And there was no one left but me.

Earlier Times – Happy Thought

The world is so full of a number of things,
I'm sure we should all be as happy as kings.

Louis – A Lover of Soap Bells

*A photograph of Louis and Charles blowing
soap bells on North Berwick Links.*

The photograph above was taken by my father, David Stevenson, in 1865. My father sensitised his plates and developed his photos right away in the harness room adjoining our stables. In those days the glass plate, one side of which he covered with a film of collodion, was then immersed in a chemical bath to sensitise it. There were no 'dry plates' and no films as we know them. Hand cameras did not exist in those days and no rapid plates either. The cap on the outside of the lens was removed by hand and replaced when the time exposure of about four seconds was deemed to be sufficient. The positives, produced after developing, were as a rule most beautiful and have lasted unfaded for many years.

The fine art of making soap bells is largely gone, so my father's photo-positive is of attractive interest especially as it shows Louis in the very act of blowing one of these lovely bells. The invasion of the wooden pipe for smokers instead of the 'cutty' with its small diameter and narrow edge is the main cause of the loss of this fine art of making soap creations. One may make a soap bell with a wooden bowl, but you cannot so deftly and so entirely dismiss the bell that may be wafted away on the gentle zephyr breeze.

The joy of creating and the wonderment as to the fate of the bells must have been of intense interest to Louis who was so keen to observe them in his young days as well as to amuse others. One can fancy Louis giving such a parody as this but in more worthy lines.

Such is not his hand:

> Oh where and oh where will my little bell go
> Oh where and oh where will it go
> To heaven above, to East or to West
> Or to God's earth below.

The pipe as mentioned in the bubble blowing is an ordinary 'cutty' or short clay pipe. The mouthpiece was most carefully covered with red sealing wax by my mother to ensure the clay did not stick to one's lips. A 'church warden' pipe, one foot in length, was much too long. The table used to rest the soap mixture on, consisted of the steps used by the maids in hanging up 'the washing' in the garden. The washing was an exceptionally large affair in our household, needed with such a number of young girls requiring spotless and bright summer dresses!

Golf

My brother and I learned to play golf from the earliest possible age and always loved the game. Indeed, Davie came to championship standard with a handicap of just four. We were members down at North Berwick and in later years the Old Luffness at Gullane, The Royal and Ancient at St Andrews and the Honourable Company of Edinburgh Golfers at Muirfield. In contrast Louis always despised this activity, instead preferring games of robbers and pirates, or just simply exploring along the coast, or journeying deep into the Lammermuir Hills; these meant much more to him.

Croquet was also fashionable at that time, but Louis felt he had something better to do than to play either croquet or golf. Croquet was often played on the North Berwick Links, but Louis seldom joined in at that time. It was much later that Louis, with Frances Sitwell in England, came to love the game and became an expert at it.

The game of croquet in those days of crinoline dresses was largely a social affair. None the less it was a game of skill, especially when the ground was by no means level. The professionally skilful, almost scientific, game as now played would never have appealed to Louis.

I once even played croquet on the Bass Rock with my sisters and the Cheynes, friends from Shetland, while on a picnic expedition, about the year 1901!

*View from Anchor Villa with the harbour entrance and Bass Rock in
the distance, circa 1860. In the foreground is the Link, with
several golfers at play. Charles seems to have been very modest as to
his own golf skills – he won the championship at North Berwick in 1882.*

Kite Flying

Apart from the soap bubbles, Louis loved to make and watch kites being wafted away in the summer breeze. There were a considerable number of other amusements that we boys shared.

Owing to the lack of amusements at Louis' home in North Berwick one may forget that they formed an integral part of Louis' young life and cannot therefore be glossed over by a mere recital of the names of such amusements.

For instance, the flying of kites was of interest to many children but was even more exciting when you were flying a kite of your own design and make; not one bought in a shop. The sending up of messages along the string up to the kite, exalted its value enormously. The adjustment of the right number of divots on the tail was a matter of significant importance to secure success.

The skilful flying of kites in all the various strengths of wind is by no means the simple matter as one might expect. The very difficulty of kite flying, when overcome, is pleasure in itself, as it is with the likes of golf, cricket and other games.

Catriona

In Louis' novel *Catriona*, Alan Breck was the accused in the Appin murder case, with a £200 reward on his head at the time of his flight with David Balfour. The story is set in the area around North Berwick, through what might have been called Louis' playground, as well as the very places where Louis and I often had played as boys. This can be of interest to those wishing to know a little more of Louis' young life.

We played on the sand hills or wreaths of sand, at the foot of the Eel Burn well known to golfers. This being the very spot where Alan Breck embarked as a fugitive, at the shore of Fidra where the eye hole in the rock is visible, at Tantallon where his hero David was a prisoner and among the bents of North Berwick where pirates, robbers and brigands were actually the game of play. So intimate are the events described in Louis' *The Pavilion on the Links* as to make these seem actually to have taken place.

The journey of David Balfour and Alan Breck from Edinburgh started as they left Silvermills in the dark and went via Broughton Street, Picardy Place and then Lochend to the Figate Whins at Portabello where they slept among the whins *(gorse)*. The two rose early next morning and had rizzored haddock, cooked on the brander with butter, for their breakfast at Musselburgh. They kept inland to Cockenzie and then stuck to the line shown on my map by way of Drem and Dirleton to the Broad Sands where they at last sighted the brig *Thistle*, which had been chartered to take Alan 'forth the country'. Louis' detailed account of Alan's embarkation is interesting:

> Then they awoke on board the Thistle and it seems as if they had all the readiness, for there was scarce a second's bustle on deck before we saw a skiff put round her stern and begin to pull lively for the coast. That part of the beach was long and flat and excellent walking when the tide was down. A little cressy burn flowed over it to the sea and the sand hills ran along the head of

it. No eye of ours should spy what was passing behind in the sand hills over which the gulls twinkled and behind which our enemies were doubtless marshalling – David said 'I have tryst to keep. I am trysted to your cousin Charlie; I have passed my word.' The captain was in the skiff himself steering. Already he was near in, and the boat was 'scouring' (a term used for the keel rubbing on the bottom). Alan immediately began to wade towards the boat. 'Davie.' he said, 'Are you no' coming. I am dead against leaving you.'

'No' a hair of me' says David. Swashing in deeper than his waist Alan was hauled into the skiff. David turned his back on the sea and faced the sand hills. There was no sound or sight of men. The sun shone on the wet sand and the dry, the wind blew in the bents, the gulls made a dreary piping. 'As I passed higher up the beach the sand-lice were hopping nimbly about the stranded tangles. At the head of the beach, I set my hat hard on my head, clenched my teeth and went right before me up the face of the wreath. It made a hard climb being steep and the sand like water underfoot. But I caught hold at last by the long bent-grass on the brae top and pulled myself to a good footing.'

David was, there and then, taken prisoner, put on horseback and taken in the dark by the south side of the Law, probably to avoid the publicity of the fishing village of North Berwick. He soon saw on the right of Whitekirk and shortly after he heard the noise of the sea.

Eventually the three huge towers and broken battlements of Tantallon Castle came into view in the moonlight. David slept in the castle under guard, yet not in the dungeon. In the dark of early morning, he was taken over in a small boat to Bass Rock as a prisoner where he remained for some time. On leaving Bass Rock his route is marked by a dotted line on my map shown earlier. Firstly, to the Lethies* where a man was put ashore and then up the Firth of Forth, between the Lamb and Craigleith and so beyond the playground.

63

*Louis' *Catriona* must then be followed to learn the end of Louis' interesting story. The spot near the Lethies where the man was put ashore was probably below the Cove in the cliffs known in our childhood as Fresh Water Bay where the drainage water from the fields above wells up as a spring through the sand. It was commonly known to nurses and children as the place the Germans had selected for their invasion of this country, this being in about 1867!

My sister Georgie asked Louis how to pronounce the name *Catriona*. 'Katrena' said Louis in three distinct syllables, at least so it sounded to me. This may have been merely Louis' pet name for our much beloved cousin Catherine de Mattos, knowing full well that there were other ways which might be more correct to be learnt but I do not know. Certain it is that Louis would have said if he had been questioned and 'what matters it', as he said in answer to other such questions related to the Scots tongue.

Summer Quarters at North Berwick

The summer home for our family, during the whole time of Louis' boyhood, was at Anchor Villa, North Berwick. Louis would spend many happy hours at our house and its garden. I believe the joyous reception he received from old and young was dear to his heart. Without the least restraint, he would eagerly enter into the numerous and varied interests of the children in our happy home as if he was one of us.

The situation of the house was ideal for golf, sea-bathing, croquet and horse riding. Perhaps Louis did not join into all these amusements, but he did seem to take general pleasure in what was going on. He loved the happiness inside the house. He adored reading, as well as smoking in the garden emitting a very marked fragrant atmosphere and wafting it around. The garden may have looked untidy, but it had redeeming features that Louis and all of us knew. It had plants carefully selected and then cultivated so as to ensure an abundant volume and delicious atmosphere never to be forgotten.

If I may trespass for a moment beyond my limited sphere of scientific engineering into the realms of the private garden. Perhaps more attention could have been bestowed on the development of honeysuckle in bushes and such like, in order to bring the modern garden to be more on a parallel with the old-time garden with its rich fragrance borne on the summer breeze instead of concentrating alone on a blaze of colour schemes.

Our house was the headquarters of the 'Lantern Bearers'; more of this later. The photographs show Anchor Villa as it was then and Louis' favourite garden seat.

*The Villa was later ruined architecturally, owing to the alterations to
make it more capacious. Indeed, it became unrecognisable and
the carved stone anchor that was above the front door had even
been hewn off. Sadly, the house in the photograph, and in which
Louis sometimes lived, is no more.*

Louis at North Berwick

The village of North Berwick and its surroundings may be said to have been perhaps the most important playground of Louis' childhood. The area of his exploits and his enjoyment was not only in his young days but also later: exploring many a ruin, castle or abbey, graveyard or quicksand. I would say these explorations was among his greatest pleasures. Often, he and I could be found playing at robbers, brigands and pirates among the bents and sand hills between North Berwick and Dirleton.

'There was nothing to mar your days if you were a boy 'summering' at North Berwick.' says Louis, 'The embarrassment of pleasures – you might golf if you wanted...' then adds, 'But, I seem to have been better employed.'

He continues 'You might secrete yourself in the Lady's Walk.'

Lady's Walk (The Glen) is a certain sunless dingle of elders all mossed over by the damp, as green as grass and dotted here and there by the stream side with roofless walls, the cold homes of anchorite recluses. To prepare themselves for life and with a special eye to acquire the art of smoking. It was even common for boys to hide themselves there.

Louis' remembrance of learning to smoke must have been vivid as he gives smoking the premier place in his pleasures of which one might partake at North Berwick! Perhaps Louis came to 'particulars', as my and his grandfather used to call it.

Louis was in his best vein giving his readers fun when describing such boys' pleasures:

'Again, you might join our fishing parties, where we sat perched as thick as solan geese, a convoy of little anglers, boy and girl, casting over each other's heads. What fun for girl and boy, this form of angling! Now infinitely superior to catching ponleys and what a lovely tangle 'with shrill recrimination, shrill as the geese themselves'

Or again you might climb the Law.

The Law is a tough little climb, although through lovely whin and grass sward between rocks was of no pleasure but rather a toil to Louis. Whereas a quick romp up the hill was a charm to other boys who adore rough and hard games such as football, cricket or tennis.

At its summit Louis states, 'You will find the whale's jawbone, stood landmark in the buzzing wind, as consolation and further you would behold the face of many counties and the smoke of many towns and the sails of distant ships!'

Louis continues, still in his inimitable style of chaff,

'You might bathe now in the flaws of fine weather, that we pathetically call our summer, now in a gale of wind, with the sand scouring your bare hide, your clothes thrashing abroad from underneath their guardian stone which anchored them temporarily while bathing. The power of the froth of the sea is extremely exhilarating, possibly one might class it as romantic – the very froth of the great breakers casting you headlong ere it had drowned your knees.'

Louis finishes by describing the lantern bearers or 'asses' as he called us. A clique of boys who had great pleasure on September evenings 'going out with the bull's eye lantern' that lit the footpaths in front of us, warned us of the edge of the bunkers on the Links or enabled us, if so desired, to cope safely by way of the gulley on the way to Campbell's Cave at Pen Garry. This was one of the meeting places of the 'Lantern Bearers', the story of which is told in biographies of Louis. David and I were old enough to join in. The gulley is seven feet deep and luckily has a stone wedge in between its sides at the top which helps one cross onto the rock with the Cave. Even in daylight passage is difficult but at night impossible without a lantern. Louis was a lantern bearer.

Louis explains in glowing humour, 'The essence of bliss was to walk by yourself in the black night and know in your 'Fool's heart' that you had a bull's eye at your belt!'

The Lantern bevy of boys, about seven or eight in number as a rule, kept their lanterns well-trimmed and serviceable, as we carried our lanterns for real use and not for make belief or silly show.

We boys sometimes went down to the Links with our lanterns and met as previously arranged at the boats on the beach. These were large herring boats, drawn up to the top of the beach in the autumn when the herring fishing had ended, to be renovated for the next year's season. One of these boats is shown in my father's photograph positive of a family gathering chiefly consisting of Louis' cousins. The boats as can be judged from the photograph were large and were drawn up by manpower, the crew of the boats helping each other. It was a major affair the hauling of these large heavy boats on roller chocks. To drag the boats on the rollers with rope and tackle, using just the backs of the anglers was quite a feat, with other helpers on each side preventing the boats from toppling over.

The boats were drawn up to the foot of the burn which then flowed past the present New Golf Club House. 'Drawing up' the herring boats was a great occasion every year. The boats did not come all together but on separate days. There was plenty of whisky supplied by the crew to those who helped. Sometimes villagers also joined in and we boys gave a hand too.

*The photograph shows one of the herring boats used
as a meeting place by the Lantern Bearers.*

Figures left to right, 'Boy 'all hands to the pumps'', Bessy my sister standing, cousin Jane, me sitting (high up), sister Mary, sister Janey (later Lady Kyllachy), unknown boy, my mother Elizabeth, finally my sister Georgie. Present but not in the photograph were my father taking the picture, Thomas and Louis, plus Coolin the dog.

I remember Louis being at one of the meetings we lantern boys had at the fishing boats. He forced his romancing to a very high pitch, or shall we say his extreme honesty of keeping nothing back by his remarks. He says that we indulged with inappropriate talk as 'indecent' and yet he says so 'innocent'.

Louis had a happy temperament, being full of fun and brightness. Generally, he was not a lover of practical jokes but here was one of his pieces of fun, which ended in near disaster. My sister and other girls used to go down to the beach on September evenings after dusk, march up and down the sands, arm in arm, singing catches which were great fun. Many were the happy hours these friends had. Louis took it into his head that he would give the young ladies some different fun, so one still night when nought was to be heard except for the occasional ripple of the sea on the sand, he got between them, and the sea and a voice was heard 'Blud'. Funny did you hear that? 'Blud – a – blud –blud – a – blud – blud – a blud' with tragic tones and spacings. One girl dashed off in a panic and then another fled and another terrified, all running off to Anchor Villa for safety. The hardier remained, in a few seconds to learn that it was only Louis who was dismayed and petrified at the unintended unhappy result.

The singing of catches by the girls were such as these:

Nay, nay don't insist
Nor bring such a list
Of grievances that don't exist
As you do now.

Or 'Ding dong bell' or 'Here lies Sir John Guise, where he's gone or how he fares no one knows and no one cares' etc. This was a very common form of amusement in girl's schools in those days.

Trip to Italy and a Missed Ball

An event happened in Louis' young life, before he was out of 'petticoat government', which certainly directed him through his young life and most probably influenced his later life. He was taken on a six months' sight-seeing tour over the continent of Europe.

As a 12-year-old child, Louis was mentally probably better equipped than most other boys would have been at that age. He already was an incessant reader of history and travelling subjects, whereas games were not his interest. My sister Bessy was in charge of the trip, which she had arranged at the request of Louis' father, Thomas. She reported that Louis physically proved to be just as fit as any of the five travellers. Louis' mother, gentle and loving as she was and who mothered him throughout his infant and childhood's usual illnesses, knew that he was quite fit for this Grand Tour especially with my sister in charge of it all. His mother would never have included her beloved 'Loo' in what she knew from her own previous experiences of travel and sight-seeing, was certain to be a severe trial of physical strength unless she had been certain that Louis was fit and well, with infant illnesses left well behind. The only illness he had of any significance while he was away on the Tour was during the two crossings of the Channel, when he was mightily ill, although the sea was anything but tempestuous.

Their Grand Tour of 1863 – culminating in Naples with its combination of frequent change of trains, carriages and hotels – was really a significant strain for all the party, combined with the demands of incessant sight-seeing over the six months.

There was a fly in the ointment as far as my sister was concerned. As a result of her absence from home on this delightful tour meant she missed 'The Royal Archers' Ball'. Each one of these social events when it came along was an episode of significant importance in a young girl's life. Bessy, being naturally at the age when to miss the Queen's Bodyguard's dance was like anathema to one. She was grievously annoyed to miss going with her sister Janey to this momentous occasion. She must have departed with a somewhat heavy heart to be missing the ball, as she had been hoping to become engaged to Alexander James Napier. She was pretty and need not to have worried, as he popped the question immediately upon her return!

Louis was too young for ball-going then and indeed he never seemed anxious to follow up the dancing lessons he had in the Quadrilles, the Lancers, the Waltz and the Polka, which were the fashionable dances in his day. Louis appreciated far more the nectar which he drew from between the dry boards of his books at home rather than precious honey from the lovely butterflies on the wing in the ballroom. This was typical of Louis and shows the spirit which leavened his whole life.

If I may digress, with a piece of my own writing *The Story of the Kiss*:

'Twas holiday morn in the Calton Ground
When Louis was studying the tombs a-round
But hush ... Yes,
'Twas a distant blow of a cherished kiss
'Twas courtly returned to the pretty miss.
And this was the end of this little story
Which was nothing to either but fun and glory'.

Charles Stevenson

Louis' Other Cousins

The following verses are from Alan Stevenson's *Hymns of Synesius*, written to his three daughters; Jane-Margaret, Catherine and Dora.

To Three Sisters

Graces from far Cambria's shore,
Sisters three of Mona's Isle:
Every motion of your lips
Is prophetic of a smile.
Countless is the changeful mirth
That illuminates your household hearth.

Margaret!* Pearl-like emblem, thou
Of a calm, kind, constant heart:
Catharina's** spotless soul
From her soft eyes seems to start.
Dora!*** Gift from heaven sent down,
Latest gem of beauty's crown

Charles added a note under this poem
*A pearl
**Pure
***Gift of God

The dresses of Aunt Jane created some interest for Louis as described in the short verse here. The dresses were made of crinoline and gave off a loud rustle.

Auntie's Dresses (Jane)

Whenever Auntie moves around
Her dresses make a curious sound
They trail behind her up the floor
And trundle after through the door.

*The photograph shows Aunt Jane with daughters Jessie and Mary
in 1861, when Louis would have been eleven years old.*

Elizabeth Stevenson, my mother had similar, with the gown having a
huge crinoline arrangement. I remember later managing to diminish its
diameter by half! This was done by cutting the steel rings with pliers and
re-splicing them. I assisted my sisters in the operation which required
considerable use of my youthful engineering skills to avoid unequal
bulging.

Louis wrote of my mother 'Her extraordinary charm and kindness, I
never saw anything like her, a look from Aunt Elizabeth was like sunshine;
she was the idol of my childhood.'

*It was most unfortunate that Charles caught diphtheria in 1871, when he
was 16, while his father was away helping with the construction of Dhu*

Heartach. His mother Elizabeth was nursing Charles, and she caught the disease and died on 7th July 1871 aged 55. This was a terrible loss to the family and Charles could never speak to anyone of his mother afterwards. Possibly he felt guilty of some sort that she had caught this illness while nursing him. Her husband recorded that it had been her final wish that none of her children were to see her as she was in death, as she wanted them to remember her as she had been in life.

Edinburgh in the 19th Century

In his boyhood, Louis had a transcendent interest in all of Edinburgh's ancient monuments, from the old City Walls to the Castle – reaching to the sky. Overtopping all of these was his interest in 'The House of Kings' as Louis poetically called the Palace of Holyrood and Arthur's Seat everchanging mood, towering high above. Louis seemed to have a kind of reverence and personal affection reaching beyond the mere historical associations of the buildings, created by the hand of man.

Louis knew every inch, from the Palace itself to the top of Arthur's Seat. The names of the lochs together with the hills and crags, were all familiar to him. Their names must have been from more than 100 years earlier. My father told me the names as having been also his own knowledge when he was a boy.

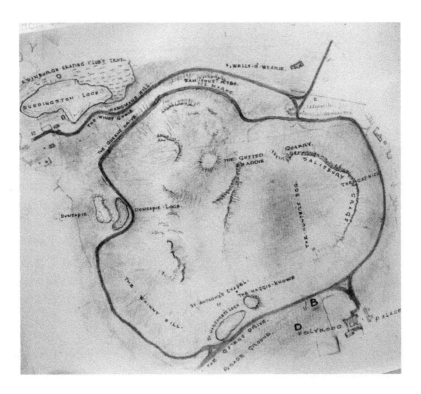

I have made a map of Arthur's Seat with the objective of helping anyone interested in the hill as Louis knew it. The mere names, as I give them are of little value in themselves, but they should be combined with a personal inspection of the hill to enable one to fully grasp the situation. I include below some notes about the hills and lochs, commencing in the neighbourhood of Holyrood and proceeding clockwise around the hill to Dunsapie, Duddington and St Leonard, then on to the foot of Salisbury Crags before returning to Holyrood and the Parade Ground.

The Haggis Knowe

This is a beautifully shaped piece of rock landscape and as such it deserves a better name. Vulcan's Laboratory did not always produce molten metal of a form and contour pleasant to the eye nor with the sweetness of curves. However, in the instance of the Haggis Knowe they have, with the Ice Eroder's powerful assistance, produced a rock far better in appearance than that of a slaughtered haggis. The Haggis Knowe, not only in its outstanding position among the surroundings of the King's Park but in its own comeliness, can never fail to be admired by all.

St Margaret's Loch

St Margaret's Loch is a small piece of water lying immediately below the Knowe and is adored by children especially in the summer.

St Anthony's Chapel

The ruins of this building lie immediately above the Loch and although of little architectural interest in themselves, they are of undoubted value in adding to the general scene from their quaint elevated position. History relates that a light was kept burning at night in the chapel to guide the ordinary wayfarer on land and to act as an indication mark for those on the sea even though it is several miles inshore. However, examination of the ruins reveals that there is nothing either left on the ground or walls to suggest that there was any tower or special window to confirm these statements.

Mushet's Cairn

A little further east is this cairn. Mushet is said to have murdered his wife near the Loch.

The Whinny Hill
Derived its name no doubt from the whins (gorse) with which it was extensively and densely covered, and which display a perfect blaze of colour for miles around when the whins are in bloom. The hill can still boast a goodly strip of whins with their lovely yellow bloom.

Dunsapie Loch
There is nothing especially spectacular about this partly artificial loch nor about the hill known as Dunsapie which overhangs the loch. The view of Arthur's Seat itself from here is somewhat tame in comparison with the views of the hill in other directions. An incident occurred here which deserves mention as it demonstrates that Louis was no exception to the rule that boys will be boys. It was suggested to me on occasion of passing the loch that there was a cave on Dunsapie known as Dirk Hatterick's Cave. There is no cave!

Probably the idea was prompted for Louis by remembrance of The Grotto known to him in Italy when he was there with my sister Bessy. The Italian word signifies light and not dark, deriving its name from the *lucus a non lucenedo* principle. Anyway, a cave was suggested when there was no cave – all in fun.

(Editor's note: Charles himself is having fun here as the 'lucus a non lucenedo' suggestion is a double pun being 'a grove from not shining' and an absurd explanation.)

If I may digress from the subject in hand, a somewhat similar incident of Louis ever at play occurred at Tantallon Castle, when he and I were together at the castle's ruins. Louis with his usual bright face came into the ruined cell where I happened to be and said something of this nature. 'Oh, come and see; I have just found some "feudal" remains.' Naturally, I at once went over to look, only to find some very recent additions but nothing 'feudal'. Such a piece of fun between us was boy-like and amusing and we both had a good laugh.

But Louis could be far more amusing and delightfully interesting with his continuous but varied repeating of tales and stories in his romancing flow of conversation. The headlines for two of his tales are *The Back of Beyond* and *The Other Side of Nowhere*.

Although the tales themselves were there and then gone, as if by magic from the wizard's wand, still we can almost scent the rich flavour of the fanciful repast which Louis had prepared for the young of heart and with which he regaled them.

Duddingston

Duddingston Loch with its surroundings is one of the most beautiful parts of the King's Park. The loveliness being enhanced by the swans with their elegant necks swimming on the loch's placid surface. In winter when the ice on the loch was strong enough to bear the weight of skaters a flag used to be hoisted on the City Chambers in Edinburgh, to inform that the loch was safe for skating. At such times skating and curling was the 'order of the day' for many people. More of this later.

The Windy Goule

On the road from Duddingston into Edinburgh there is a narrow and twisted gorge called the Windy Goule between Hangman's Hill and the heights of Arthur's Seat, well named indeed as in the very lightest of breezes one finds a gale passing through the gorge. An iron handrail has added greatly to the safety of people walking through the gorge.

Wells O'Wearie

A little further on lies the Wells O'Wearie, which for many a day have supplied an abundance of water not only for the cattle and other farm use but also for the brewery.

Samson's Ribs

Overhanging the lower road are Samson's Ribs, a rock of basalt columns with rib-like convex curvature. Some sections of the columns found on the surface of the ground 18 and 20 miles east of Samson's Ribs suggest they came from Arthur's Seat with the ice.

Ice Markings

At the side of the Queen's Drive above the Ribs are evident marks of the passage of the ice cap which flowed from West to East. The ice, with stones and sand embedded in it, very largely moulded the country to its present configuration by wearing away the softer rocks and leaving the harder rocks.

The Echoing Rock
The Echoing Rock is the next place of note in our circular tour around Arthur's Seat. It is a rock face on the side of the hill and if you stand opposite the face and shout loudly, wafting back is the echo of your call, in a fascinating perfect replication of your voice.

The Gutted Haddie
Nearby is another route to climb Arthur's Seat but it involves a rather difficult piece of steep climbing sufficient to deter all but the hardiest from ascending the hill from this side.

The Gutted Haddie derives its name from the structure of a rock face resembling that of fish bones.

Salisbury Crags
The Salisbury Crags form a most attractive piece of rock scenery, given the combined work of 'Vulcan' and the 'Ice Eroder', well worthy of even more majestic praise than their work at Haggis Knowe.

The Cat Nick
This is the only break in the otherwise long line of precipitous cliffs of Salisbury Crags. The Nick is a cleft with more difficult rock work for the climber than the Gutted Haddie. The Nick has often been ascended both by men and boys.

And now having gone all round the hill back to Holyrood and the Parade Ground one must not forget the Hunter's Bog sunk in the very heart of Arthur's Seat. This is the name given to the grassy hollow which lies between the hill itself and Salisbury Crags. It has been wisely utilized for many a long day as a series of rifle ranges. If things had been otherwise the Hunter's Bog could have been a most attractive valley as it lies north and south, therefore being well sheltered from the prevailing winds by the hill and the Crags.

The King's Park

The glory of the King's Park – may its glory ever reign supreme! There never was a blot on the escutcheon of the King's Park. One of the most interesting parts of the King's Park is the Parade Ground; a nearby level piece of ground extending to many acres, ideal for drilling soldiers. In Louis' younger days the soldiers from the Castle were marched down the streets with the band playing – a most invigorating combination and to some people even becoming captivating, resulting in recruitment, encouraged by the boom from the best of the big drum.

Louis fond of marching gusto, for him the very heart springs, the action of the drummer, the fibres of the muscles all astir producing a thrill which Louis evidently felt for he joined in, sometimes marching alongside for a while.

On account of better and more extensive accommodation elsewhere for the troops from the Castle and the barracks at Jock's Lodge, the Parade and the streets are now free from daily military use.

The Parade Ground remains of value to the nation as is evidenced by the fact that it has been the scene of two great Review of Troops, in my lifetime. The first being in 1881 with the Review by her Majesty Queen Victoria, of volunteers from England (six counties) and from Scotland (every county). The second Great Review being in June 1946 when their Majesties the King and Queen held a great review of the British Legion of Scotland to celebrate the first anniversary of Victory Day.

No wonder this spot was chosen for reviews, for is it not a remarkable site – the Palace of Holyrood – Arthur's Seat towering high above – the natural setting of the hillside forming a sloping platform of enormous size – the Haggis Knowe – St Margaret's Loch, the ruins of St Anthony's Chapel and Salisbury Crags. All join in forming a parade ground that is unequalled in the land. This within 10 minutes' drive of the centre of Princes Street by the Royal Mile or by Robert Stevenson's lovely cist of the Great North Road to London, having the most fascinating uninterrupted views of Arthur's Seat and Salisbury Crags and on a road of graceful curves and 'graded' most beautifully.

Her Majesty, the late Queen Victoria, escorted by a Troop of the 21st Hussars left Holyrood Palace, or as Louis called The Palace House of Kings, at about 3.45pm, in a 'Victoria' carriage and four grey horses and two outriders also on greys. The reason it was a 'Victoria' was no doubt to make the getting in and out easier for the Queen. A Battery of the Royal Artillery stationed on the Queen's Drive at the same time gave a Royal Salute of 21 guns.

The Volunteer Cavalry Brigade, which was drawn up opposite the entrance to the Palace, was inspected by her Majesty. She then inspected the rest of the Volunteer Force, before proceeding to the Saluting Flag erected near the centre of the Parade Ground. At the flag was the Guard of Honour, men of the Royal Company of Archers, The Queen's Bodyguard for Scotland.

The Edinburgh Skating Club

The Edinburgh Skating Club, which was founded in 1642 but may have been in existence even earlier, made 'Duddingston' their headquarters. In Louis' early days the club might well have been said to be the Institution of the King's Park itself and Royalty graced the Club with their name. Although Louis was never a member of the Club, he knew many of the members. These included Fleeming Jenkins and James Simpson, both splendid skaters.

The members skated in tall hats, dressed in morning tailcoat, waistcoat and formal trousers and wore the club medal with the Prince of Wales' feathers. The club was very exclusive, as even one single black ball in the ballot excluded membership. But what made membership even more difficult was that in order to join a skater on trial had to jump over a row of tall hats, with their own on top! The club tests were strict. I passed all the difficult tests when I was 24 years old in 1879 and my brother David the same year. Later, I wrote a pamphlet titled *Statistics and dynamics of ice skating* that incorporated the club rules, usually forgotten between one generation and the next. My father had it privately printed, and it sold well. Before the turn of the century, I was one of only two British skaters qualified to judge the gold medallists of the day. Skating had been a big part of our lives since my grandfather Robert's day.

In Edinburgh we had freezing winters every year between 1879 and 1889 lasting for almost six weeks. During the skating season a tent was pitched on the south side of the Loch, usually in a kind of oasis of reeds for the use of members of the club. The Officer of the club wore a long dark blue great coat or 'Ulster' with red collar and brass buttons.

Louis, although a skater could never be induced to practice sufficiently to be a member of the club. The result was that he skated alone ploughing his own furrows through the snow besmirched the glassy surface of the frozen loch instead of having the company of other boys and girls of his own age, in skating on the loch. He could manage to do little twists and turns within a two-foot compass, which seemed to give him much satisfaction and pleasure. I gave Louis the loan of a pair of skates during the skating season. Referring to skating Louis wrote the following letter to Cousin Bob in 1877:

'A fortnight's frost and I have skated every afternoon – I can't skate more; I make some progress and do some back things smaller and faster than my fellow countrymen generally, but as what they hanker after is bigness and slowness and ever a greater protraction of the leg, that is perhaps not much to boast of.'

As a matter of history our grandfather, Robert, used skates made out of bone but 50 years or so later we were using hollow grounded steel blades. The Old Edinburgh Skating Club then adopted the English style of skating. At the time of writing, the secretary of the club is my son D. Alan Stevenson.

The sanctity of the Edinburgh Skating Club's ring on Duddingston was marked merely by a ring of swept snow and was evidenced by the fact that police assistance was never required to keep the club's ring clear of the public skaters. The obvious ability of the club skaters to do acrobatic feats on ice with perfect ease and grace, while maintaining the power of keeping time in their combined kaleidoscopic skating, struck the public with amazement and wonder, all done without any apparent strain. This was sufficient together with the skater's tall hats and dress to ensure that never a single skater from the public throng ventured to pass across the sacred ring of snow!

'Good form' was imperative, and onlookers were astonished to see the effect of eight fine skaters performing around a small circle in the centre of the ring and then all simultaneously gliding off noiselessly and smoothly without exertion to the boundary of the ring. This before returning back to the centre being like a daisy flower opening up and then closing.

The Edinburgh Skating Club are well justified in retaining the motto *'Ocior Euro'* on the club's medal, which translates as 'swifter than the wind'. Do they not in a flash change from all being at a centre, to all being at the outer limit of their ring in a mere moment? And this without even a flutter of garment, in fact without the wind having time to act!

Charles and Robert Scott-Moncrieff performing 'Cupid' on Duddingston Loch.

The Bugle Call and its Revival

In our younger days Edinburgh Castle would sound out the Bugle call at six o'clock in the morning and this could be clearly heard from Heriot Row by Louis. The sight of soldiers marching with their band playing, swinging down from the castle to Jock's Lodge always affected us deeply and we stopped to watch them go by. With a Highland regiment the kilts would swing almost imperceptibly and on a recruiting march, the music to some light air as 'The girl I left behind....' Then would set off marching alongside them admiring the action of the drummer and the strong muscle of the men.

This bugle call is not now sounded as the troops are long gone from the castle. However, it would be useful in the present day if the system of bugle call could be revived as it would be a constant reminder to the tourists and holiday makers of the hour, with the gentle notes of the bugle.

A Comparison of Homelife

In order to give one an idea of what kind of life Louis had in which to move, I give a description of the house that my father had in the Royal Terrace. Louis often came to our house in his boyhood when he was old enough to go about on his own, clear of nursery domination. Life in my house with six children differed so very greatly from that of Louis' family, consisting of a solitary son. There was always someone at home to give him time and attention, often with much music and song. The hustle and bustle with happy play and excitement of ours, contrasting with the monotony of Louis' own home. It is perhaps no wonder that Louis came as often as he did to the Royal Terrace from Herriot Row despite it being a longish walk back and forth, unaccompanied by brothers or sisters.

Sometimes Louis would break in his walk to peep into Smith's, the stationer's shop at the corner of Antigua Street on his way. This shop was patronized by the Edinburgh Academy boys, as it stocked all the requisites for school. More unusually it had model theatres and the scripts for plays, printed on poor-quality paper, the figurines of actors on large pasteboard sheets which had to be cut out, being either coloured or uncoloured. There were tin 'spoons' as we called them, for mounting the figures upon long stiff wire. These could then be used to manoeuvre the models around the stage as required, in order to re-enact the play. The wings were crudely painted, and the background scenes were also sold at Smith's shop.

By contrast the model theatre at our house seemed a very superior affair, to anything that was on the market at Smith's or elsewhere. The stage was large, complete with trapdoor. There was an arrangement for the rapid change of wings and scenes, together with a drop curtain on pulleys. The whole construction including side boxes, was designed and built by my father. We also had a fine peep show with an 8-inch diameter lens and mirror.

The whole atmosphere of our house and garden, seemed to be enjoyed by Louis – being full of life both inside and out. He would always receive a warm greeting from my parents and us children, being two boys and four girls. The quiet management of the family by my parents was perhaps the main thing which must have appealed to Louis.

A simple example perhaps explains the method of bringing up children without a trace of disquiet. Inscribed in pencil inside the backboard of a Walker's Dictionary the following written by an elder sister, 'Mamma has said no, so please don't ask again.' Such quiet methods characterized the whole dealings of our parents with their children in all difficulties.

Louis from his early boyhood often was found to be at our home, his uncle and aunt's house. The father and mother were the mainspring of our home, the father worshipping the mother and the mother likewise worshipping the father. My parents had known each other from their own childhood and had often played together, although there was no family tie. When David was 18 years old and Elizabeth 14 years old, they were carving their initials on a tree on the banks of the River Forth at Stirling. When Bessy was 18, she was sending her silhouette, made by August Edouart, to David. On the reverse of the silhouette is written:

To D.S.
From his ever devoted and affectionate,
Bessy 21st Feb 1837

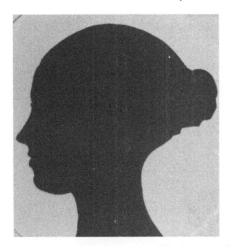

Elizabeth and David.

No wonder Louis adored my mother with her infectious smile, which reflected throughout her life, together with generous and gentle thoughts. Printed notes prepared by my father show the wealth of love which adorned the lives of the two; devoted David and the no less devoted Elizabeth.

Sweet-voiced angels seemed to roam around them in their happy home.

25 Royal Terrace, Edinburgh

For a long time, my father's house was 25 Royal Terrace, Edinburgh. Our home being one of those four storied houses built of Craigleith sandstone on the east side of the city, being very well suited to accommodate a large family, so common in those days. As Louis was a frequent visitor to the house I give here a rough idea of the garden, in which we often played.

The garden was really a glorified back green. It was well sheltered by the high houses from northerly winds and from all southerly winds by the Calton Hill with its wooded northern slope. Easterly and westerly winds affected us little as most of the garden was walled, so much so that even in winter it seemed a veritable 'Riviera' when the sun shone. We could turn either to the right or left at the end of the garden in Royal Terrace and by following one of the many paths, laid around the Calton Hill by our grandfather Robert after the soldiers had returned from the Napoleonic wars, we would arrive at Waterloo Place – having the east end of Princes Street. Years later Louis was to write in Samoa, remembering the family graves at the New Calton Cemetery in Edinburgh:

The tropics vanish and me seems that I,
From Halkerside, from topmost Allermuir,
Or steep Caerketton, dreaming gaze again.
Far set in fields and woods, the town I see
Springs gallant from the shallows of her smoke,
Cragged spired and turreted, her virgin fort Beflagged.
About, on seaward-drooping hills,
New folds of city glitter.
Last the Forth Wheels ample waters set with secret isles,
And populous Fife smokes with a score of towns.

There, on the sunny frontage of a hill,
Hard by the house of kings repose the dead,
My dead, the ready and the strong of word,

Their works, the salt-encrusted, still survive.
The sea bombards their founded towers, the night
Thrills pierced with their strong lamps. The artificers,
One after one, here in this gated cell,
Where the rain erases and the rust consumes.
Fell upon lasting silence. Continents
And continental oceans intervene.
A sea uncharted, on a lampless isle,
Environs and confines their wandering child
In vain. The voice of generations dead
Summons me sitting distant, to arise,
My numerous footsteps nimbly to retrace,
And all mutations over, stretch me down
In that denoted city of the dead.

The gated cell in the cemetery is the only one to retain its original roof. Robert used the same method in its construction, of 'dovetailing' the stones into each other, that he had employed in the building of the Bell Rock Lighthouse.

In the garden at Royal Terrace there was a prominent set of steps that we children used for assorted games. One game christened by Louis was a variation of rounders with a long rope extending across the garden he called the Rope of Good Hope which he liked to pronounce as the 'Roup of Good Houp.' The rope had to be negotiated at the finish, with the stone steps needing to be ascended and descended on tip toe stepping on upturned flowerpots with one on each step. To the youngest, the rules and regulations of this game were so elaborate as to be beyond the whit of man!

In the centre of the garden was a large stone water bath surrounded by a rockery. It had a model flour mill made of tin, complete with mill lade and water wheel.

Near the top of the garden was a second rockery. Both rockeries had an assortment of stones some of which had been sent to my father from the Isle of Man, these being of quartz with crystals studded over them which glittered charmingly.

The top rockery bore a smooth stone of a wondrous curved shape named by Louis as The Pool of Siloam, with its smooth hollow top. This was possibly a relic from the Stone Age. In rainy weather it filled with water from the heavens, but which mysteriously was often found full in dry weather and almost overflowing when the weather seemed to be tropical.

The hollowed shape could have been described by that great engineer Leonardo di Vinci as having a parabolic curve. The phenomenon or origin of the curve was somewhat difficult to explain away or to gloss over to the uninitiated.

At the top of the garden was a trellis arbour with unusual glazed hollow bricks for the floor. The hollows were used for a time as 'hidey holes' for our tobacco pipes when it was supposed that we did not know anything about smoking. But didn't we know? Only too well sometimes!

A large elm tree at the top of the garden was exceedingly difficult to climb even for me – the best of the climbers. It was ascended at times by a rope ladder of my own design and construction.

The garden plots were filled with gillyflowers (stocks) and roses, honeysuckle, snowdrops, moss-roses, geranium and foxgloves. It was a regular old-fashioned garden with walls covered with wisteria, cotoneaster, also there were a few willows and lime trees. The end of the top garden opened into the semi-public garden area with lovely wide-open views to Arthur Seat, North Berwick Law and the coast of Fife with the Firth of Forth – a garden unequalled in the city of Edinburgh in my opinion.

The drawback for me to this house, was its long distance from the Edinburgh Academy. By contrast, Louis at 17 Heriot Row was but a stone's throw away from the school.

Melville Street – Another Stevenson Home

It was perhaps good fortune that the three Stevenson brothers – Alan, David and Thomas –maintained an unbroken friendship, thus avoiding family restrictions. It would therefore be almost endless to relate all the happy meetings one had with Louis.

However, one particular occasion sticks in my mind when Louis and Cousin Bob were calling at our house in Melville Street. Both boys were fond of music and often demanded performances from family members. My sister Mary played the harp, an instrument which Louis adored, and sister Georgie played accompaniment on the piano, all with excellent effect. During this particular performance, we heard a noise of cymbals from the street. Upon looking out of the drawing room window, to the delight of Louis and Bob, we saw two men in blue with a stout pole and a dancing bear on a leash. The two cousins were in ecstasy over the bear and danced in the window recesses imitating the lumbering manner of the bear to the clash of the cymbals. Money was sent down which was evidentially appreciated as the men gave a second performance which we had asked for. Louis and Bob, my sisters and I enjoyed these few minutes of excitement and yet I am sure we were all sorry for the poor bear – a captive in adversity.

The drawing room in which Mary is seen playing the harp in my photograph, was one of the delightful rooms into which the sun would stream, from early morn till late in the afternoon and required sun blinds on all the windows to keep the room cool in summertime. There was a large mirror at each end of the room, a grand piano, a large draught screen, many easy chairs, a lovely marble fireplace and lots of pictures to make it homely, together with a blazing coal fire in winter months.

The house was lit by gas with chandeliers and sidelights and being heated by what was then very up to date, namely stoves and gas fires.

At the top of the house, I had a combined laboratory and workshop. I had a turning lathe which was worked by an electric motor of my own design. I also had a home-made spectroscope which gave very perfect lines, photographic equipment, chemical apparatus for making gunpowder and fireworks, gas for explosives and lead gear for making bullets for catapults. Then a home invented seismograph for showing tremors in storms and earthquakes. I collected the lead from the neighbour's roof flashings, that seemed to me to be unnecessarily deep! Also, a host of other items I will not list here.

I mention a few of these things to show that Louis as a boy had many items of an engineering nature before him, to see and examine if he had so wished. However, nothing at all of an engineering nature was of real interest to him.

However, Louis and Bob did show interest in the pictures and paintings that my father had collected over time, both in this country and abroad. He had Turner's watercolour of the Bell Rock Lighthouse and Sam Bough's watercolour of 'North Unst', as well as a lovely skating scene by Klein. As a collector of prints he had a fine line engraving of the 'Laughing Artist' by Bloemaeart.

There was another picture and an exceedingly rare one, which is of an Amsterdam canal scene, being an engraving by the 18th century artist Jonas Zeuner. The medium is unusual; silver and gold are engraved on the reverse of the glass surface just like mirror in both cases. In the picture the water is depicted as silver as are the town houses. The boats and trees are depicted in gold as is the town hall clock and the drawbridge across the canal. The sky is painted in a delightful natural colour with dramatic cloud. The picture frame being mounted on pivots so that it could readily be slewed up and down to produce the wondrous effect of night and day at will, merely by moving the frame. It is a lovely piece of workmanship and engraving – a marvel to Louis and Bob.

Verre Eglomise painting on glass by Jonas Zeuner (1727–1824).
The frame remains intact, but the pivots no longer exist.

Verre Eglomise comes from the French term meaning 'glass gilded'. It is a process where the reverse side of a piece of glass is gilded with gold or silver leaf using a gelatine adhesive. The result is a mirror-like, softly reflective surface that when combined with reverse painting techniques creates rich, shimmering and beautifully reflective pieces of artwork. The technique requires the artist to create an image in reverse order.

The artist applies the gilding and highlights first, then creates the background image on top of the highlights.

There are number of late 18th-century examples depicting views of Holland produced by the Dutch artist signing himself simply as 'Zeuner'. He was Jonas Zeuner (1727–1814) and was active in Amsterdam for a good many years.

The picture in the Stevenson's house was by Zeuner showing a view from Ridderbrug across the Oude Scans towards the north-east overlooking the Kikkerbilsluis, the Gravenhekje to the right and the Montelbaans Toren to the left.

Louis as a Companion

Whether he was on the streets, on the bents, in the house or at the dinner table, Louis was a grand companion as he was interested in everything. He could not pass a beggar on the street without giving them some money.

One of the chief enjoyments of Louis' life was having a chat. It could be with a forester, a carter, a haymaker, a man breaking stones at the side of the road, an angler at the harbour, a fishwife baiting the hooks with mussels, or a gamekeeper with gun and game bag. Everyone at work for him was a mine of information. What was a real advantage to Louis was that he seemed to make them all pleased and loquacious by his pronunciation and his choice of words when speaking to each. This ability of Louis endeared him at once to those with whom he spoke, no matter what their station. This was a marked skill of his even from an early age, being one of his great pleasures in life.

His cousin Bob was a most loveable man. He gave my father three of his beautiful paintings, all oils; one of a man walking through Fontainebleau, one of a bridge at Grez and one a river scene on the Upper Thames with a small but vivid touch of red in the distance. Whether these pictures were gifts, I don't know. They might have been in return for the canoe my father gave to Bob when he was at Cambridge and possibly in return for the financial assistance Bob received from my father to carry him through his university expenses.

These two cousins, Louis and Bob, were lifelong friends. They had many things in common, their spirit for exploring and moving about, together with a love for writing. Perhaps a difference could be found in Bob's eye for an image. Bob would see beauty in a salmon fisherman's barrel of tar for rope. Besmearing round and round with the tar slowly creeping down and the sun gleaming and reflecting rays of sunlight from so many surfaces. This could be sufficient for the artist in Bob to paint an entrancing picture, for which most would see as a distinctly unsavoury and uninviting object to choose as subject matter. The wondrous light and shade were of absorbing interest and value to Bob, whereas the fisherman's barrel would be passed and discarded by Louis as quickly as possible.

From a Railway Carriage

Below, is a poem written shortly after a day out together when Louis and I sat at the window seats of a railway carriage between Bridge of Allan and Edinburgh. Every now and then, as we were whisked along in the railway train and occasionally whistled through a station, he would ask, 'Can you get anything to rhyme with cart/horse/lump/screech' and so on.

Faster than fairies, faster than witches,
Bridges and houses, hedges and ditches.
All through the meadows the horses and cattle.
All of the sights of the hill and the plain
Fly as thick as driving rain.
And ever again, in the wink of an eye,
Painted stations whistle by.

Here is a child who clambers and scrambles
All by himself and gathering brambles.
Here is a tramp who stands and gazes.
And there is the green for stringing the daisies!
Here is a cart run away in the road
Lumping along with man and load.
And here is a mill and there is a river.
Each a glimpse and gone for ever!

For ever and anon as the train rushed on, a new sight caught Louis' interest. Each and all of the occurrences momentarily seen by us were as if photographed in Louis' mind and were duly recorded by him at the time.

Everything described happened during that journey – the lumping of a horse and cart, the shimmer of rain, all burned into my memory. More so than many of the hundred and one times in which we were together.

Some of these are tantalisingly evanescent; only few so clear to me as on this occasion.

Louis was composing and writing all the time on our train journey. A wonderful composition he has given, making one feel as if you were on the train, in rapid motion and had been not only eye but also ear witness to the events.

And More of Louis

In 1870 Louis had been on a three-week trip to Earraid (off Mull) to see the construction of the Dhu Heartach lighthouse. It was a while later that he wrote a fulsome piece of what he saw and experienced there, being a lively account of the project.

It might surprise people to know that Louis made a considerable number of visits to locations where lighthouses and other civil engineering constructions were taking place, sometimes accompanying his father. Before Louis had been to Earraid, he visited two other engineering works then in progress by the family firm. There was Dunoon on the Clyde (the main seaport in Scotland), to witness a wooden pier in the course of construction; he also visited a concrete breakwater construction in Fife.

He stayed at Wick for a while where he saw the stone and concrete development in progress there, which involved a good deal of diving. To descend in a diving suit is no part of an engineer's duties but Louis had a fancy to be dressed as a diver in the diving suit. He dressed and was taken down by Bain the head diver. It is no joyride to get dressed in extra warm clothing and pull on the heavy waterproof suit with its brass collar, finally to have the helmet screwed on with its glass window porthole, fixed upon your head and then to descend the ladder into the sea. Coming back out of the water after the dive is no mean feat either; the climb back up the long ladder wearing heavy weighted boots and lead blocks attached to your chest and back, all with the very heavy helmet. This provides an indication of Louis' strength and stamina. He described his experience beneath the water in his work *'Further Memories.'*

It interested me to watch the divers in their work at Wick. Although deep, the water was clear, and one could see the divers' movements very distinctly. The divers on coming up brought up a small variety of luminaria which they ate apparently with much relish. To be able to say that one has been down in a diving suit would never have been sufficient inducement to me to dress and go down in such a weird and disagreeable diving apparatus. For me it is somewhat like the human body 'fearfully and wonderfully made' and yet so different from the diving bell, which by comparison was simple but of much less use in comparison with this modern diving suit. In my extensive experience as an engineer I neither found it necessary nor advisable to go down.

It seems to me that one particular episode in Louis' life finally made him determined to forsake any idea of becoming a lighthouse engineer. It happened upon a voyage he made with his father while inspecting a number of lighthouses. The voyage was one of many days duration with rough seas endured before reaching the Shetland Isles, followed by a passage to Fair Isle and then on to Sumburgh Head through the Sumburgh Roost. Even in quiet weather the tidal races, or 'roosts', run strong. Sometimes as high as seven knots, so much so that a ship's motion is generally too severe for a landsman. With even the least wind, many a man has wished the ship would go to the bottom.

Louis' Theatricals

Louis loved theatricals and theatrical dress. The theatricals held by Professor and Mrs Jenkin in their house at Great Stuart Street in Edinburgh were of great pleasure to him. Fleeming Jenkins was Professor of Engineering at Edinburgh University from 1868 to 1885. Louis, David and I all became members of his university class: Louis in 1867, next David in 1871 and then myself in 1872. The essay Louis wrote about Fleeming Jenkins, showed the importance of their special relationship in shaping a large part of Louis' life.

Many a time I was at these theatricals. The plays in themselves for my part were too high brow. I went solely to see Louis and meet the audience! I could not really say whether Louis was a good actor or not; my purpose was principally to see Louis. Socially it was always a pleasure to meet the audience, so many of them being family friends.

For these theatricals Louis would dress in elaborate and apparently costly garments and wigs. During his boyhood and throughout his life he had a love for dressing up in the unusual. For instance, he desired to be photographed say as a rider, an angler, a writer, as a robber on the beach or a pirate. I remember he wanted to dress at Lerwick in the Shetland Isles in a spray gown. At Wick he carried this craze to his utmost pitch in the diver's suit except for the red cowl. The cowl cap on the diver's head would reach down to the eyebrows, which gave the unfortunate appearance of giving the wearer the appearance of having a blood-stained brow, a blood curdling look never to be forgotten!

Theatricals, a term that has fallen out of common usage, is defined in the Cambridge dictionary as performances by people untrained or not paid to act but who practice and perform in the time when they are not working.

America

Perhaps to reflect Louis restless spirit, Charles drew this pencil sketch of the American flag as a precede to this short poem composed by Louis. The poem poetically draws on the familial link between Britain and the USA.

In the States

With half a heart I wonder here
As from an age gone by
A brother – yet though young in years,
An elder brother I.

You speak another tongue than mine
Though both were English born
I towards the night of time decline
You mount into the morn.

You shall grow great and strong and free,
But age must still decay:
Tomorrow for the States – for me,
England and Yesterday

Preface to Louis' Scots Poems

To suit the present-day reader, it seems as well to introduce here a translation of some of Louis' Scots poems. Owing to the number of old Scottish words and phrases in existence these poems can be quite unintelligible to the English reader of today. Many years have passed, and many things have happened since they were written to make translation advisable.

It can be a mistake to presume that what Louis wrote accurately reflects his own nature. I believe it is wrong to form a conclusion, even from his letters. Louis in his early days was a romancer to the backbone.

His mother and he knew that all his letters would likely at some time become public property and indeed they perhaps were written to suit the palate of the outside reader.

The Maker to Posterity

Far b'yons among the years to be,
When all we think and all we see
And all we love's been knocked aside
By time's rough shoulder,
And what was right and wrong for me
Lies mangl'd all together.

I's possible – It's hardly more –
That some one, groping after learning –
Some old professor or young heir,
If still there's either –
May find and read me and be sore
Perplexed, poor brother!

'What tongue does your old buukie speak?'
He will ask; and I, his mouth to close:
Not being fir to write in Greek,
I wrote in Lallan*
Dear to my heart as peat-reeek**
Old as Tantallon***

Few spake it then and now there's none.
My poor old songs lie all their own
Their sense that once was clear alone
Lost all together
Like words upon a standing stone
Among the heather –

But think not you the hill to speed.
You too, must chew the bitter feed
For all your learning and your skill,
You are none so lucky.
And things are maybe worse than well
For you my buckie!

The whole concern (both hens and eggs,
Both books and writers, stars and clegs)****
Now staggers upon loosened legs
And wears away:
The most of mankind, near the dregs,
Runs very low.

Your book, that in some fine new tongue
You wrote or printed, preached or sung,
Will still be just a child and young
In fame and years,
When the whole planet's guts are flung
About your ears.

And you, gripping hard to a spar
Or o'erturned with some blazing star
Crying to know where the dev'l you are,
Home, France, or Flanders –
Fly in pieces like a railway car
And fly in cinders.

To help by way of explanation and context the following may be of assistance:

> *Lowlands as opposed to the tongue of the Highlands of Scotland.
> **Peat-reek is smoke from burning peat but often when the peat is burning properly there is not a trace of smoke and yet the lovely smell of burning peat, dear to my heart.
> ***Tantallon Castle, an ancient ruin in East Lothian. The Red Douglas family held it long and made it impregnable being 180 feet above sea level.
> ****A kind of fly which annoys horses and cattle.

At North Berwick Law

It was quite a tough climb for Louis to reach the top of North Berwick Law but he did it often enough. There had been a memorably bright moonlit night he remembered when he wrote this poem in 1887:

A Mile and a Bittock

A mile an' a bittock, a mile or twa,
Abune the burn, ayont the law,
Davie an' Donal' an' Cherlie an' a',
An' the mune was shinin' clearly!

Ane went hame wi' the ither, an' then
The ither went hame wi' the ither twa men,
An' baith wad return him the service again,
An' the mune was shinin' clearly!

The clocks were chappin' in house an' ha',
Eleeven, twal an' ane an' twa;
An' the guidman's face was turnt to the wa',
An' the mune was shinin' clearly!

A wind got up frae affa the sea,
It blew the stars as clear's could be,
It blew in the een of a' o' the three,
An' the mune was shinin' clearly!

Noo, Davie was first to get sleep in his head,
'The best o' frien's maun twine,' he said;
'I'm weariet, an' here I'm awa' to my bed.'
An' the mune was shinin' clearly!

Twa o' them walkin' an' crackin' their lane,
The mornin' licht cam gray an' plain,
An' the birds they yammert on stick an' stane,
An' the mune was shinin' clearly!

O years ayont, O years awa',
My lads, ye'll mind whate'er befa'-
My lads, ye'll mind on the bield o' the law,
When the mune was shinin' clearly.

The photographs are of North Berwick Law and Charles with his pony.

Charles added the following as a footnote:

The whole story is a romance roughly founded on what took place as boys playing together on the shelter or 'bield' of North Berwick Law. Donald was my pony. The first line of Verse 6 in English would read:

Two of them (Louis and Charles) walking and talking alone.

The Fortune Teller

O, I would like to know – to the beggar-wife says I –
Why chops are good to grill and none so good to fry.
And money, that is so good to keep, is better still to give.
It is very easy asking, says to beggar-wife to me.

O, I would like to know – to the beggar-wife says I –
Now all things come to be where we find them when we try,
The lasses in their clothes and the fishes in the sea.
It is very easy asking, says the beggar-wife to me.

O, I would like to know, to the beggar-wife says I –
Why lads are all to sell and the lasses all to buy:
And nobody for decency but barely two or three.
It is very easy asking, says the beggar-wife to me.

O, I would like to know, to the beggar-wife says I –
If death is as sure to as killing is to kye,*
Why God has filled the earth so full of tasty things to press.
It is very easy asking, says the beggar-wife to me.

O, I would like to know, to the beggar-wife says I –
The reason of the cause and therefore of the why,
Why many another riddle brings the tear into my eye.
It is very easy asking, says the beggar-wife to me.

*Cattle pronounced as the two last letter of the word sky

The Counter Blast Ironical

It's strange that God should fash to frame
The yearth and lift sae hie,
An' clean forget to explain the same
To a gentleman like me.

They gutsy, donnered ither folk,
Their weird they weel may dree;
But why present a pig in a poke*
To a gentleman like me?

They ither folk their parritch eat
An' sup their sugared tea;
But the mind is no to be wyled wi' meat
Wi' a gentleman like me.

They ither folk, they court their joes**
At gloamin' on the lea;
But they're made of a commoner clay, I suppose,
Than a gentleman like me.

They ither folk, for richt or wrang,
They suffer, bleed, or dee;
But a' thir things are an emp'y sang
To a gentleman like me.

It's a different thing that I demand,
Tho' humble as can be –
A statement fair in my Maker's hand
To a gentleman like me:

A clear account writ fair an' broad,
An' a plain apologie;
Or the deevil a ceevil word to God
From a gentleman like me.

*An impossible problem
**Lovers
***Die is pronounced 'dee' in Scots

115

Table of Common Scottish Vowel Sounds

ae a'	open A as in rare
au aw	AW as in law
ea	open E as in mere but this with exceptions, as heather = heather, wean=wain, lear=lair.
ee ei ie	open E as in mere
oa	open O as in more
ou	doubled O as in poor
ow	OW as in bower
u	doubled O as in poor
ui or u-umlaut before R	(say roughly) open A as in rare
ui or u-umlaut before any other consonant	(say roughly) close I as in grin
y	open I as in kite
i	pretty nearly what you please, much as in English. But in Scots it dodges usually from the short I, as in grin, to the open E, as in mere

A Lowden Sabath Morn

The clinkum-clank o' Sabbath bells
Noo to the hoastin' rookery swells,
Noo faintin' laigh in shady dells,
Sounds far an' near,
An' through the simmer kintry tells
Its tale o' cheer.

An' noo, to that melodious play,
A deidly awn the quiet sway –
A' ken their solemn holiday,
Bestial an' human,

The singin' lintie on the brae,
The restin' plou'man.

He, mair than a' the lave o' men,
His week completit joys to ken;
Half-dressed, he daunders out an' in,
Perplext wi' leisure;
An' his raxt limbs he'll rax again
Wi' painfu' pleesure.

The steerin' mither strang afit
Noo shoos the bairnies but a bit;
Noo cries them ben, their Sinday shuit
To scart upon them,
Or sweeties in their pouch to pit,
Wi' blessin's on them.

The lasses, clean frae tap to taes,
Are busked in crunklin' underclaes;
The gartened hose, the weel-filled stays,
The nakit shift,
A' bleached on bonny greens for days,
An' white's the drift.

An' noo to face the kirkward mile
The guidman's hat o' dacent style,
The blackit shoon, we noon maun fyle
As white's the miller:
A waefu' peety tae, to spile
The warth o' siller.

Our Marg'et, aye sae keen to crack,
Douce-stappin' in the stoury track,
Her emeralt goun a' kiltit back
Frae snawy coats,
White-ankled, leads the kirkward pack
Wi' Dauvit Groats.

A thocht ahint, in runkled breeks,
A' spiled wi' lyin' by for weeks,
The guidman follows closs, an' cleiks
The sonsie misses;
His sarious face at aince bespeaks
The day that this is.

And aye an' while we nearer draw
To whaur the kirkton lies alaw,
Mair neebours, comin' saft an' slaw
Frae here an' there,
The thicker thrang the gate, an' caw
The stour in air.

But hark! the bells frae nearer clang
To rowst the slaw, their sides they bang
An' see! black coats a'ready thrang
The green kirkyaird;
And at the yett, the chestnuts spang
That brocht the laird.

The solemn elders at the plate
Stand drinkin' deep the pride o' state:
The practised hands as gash an' great
As Lords o' Session;
The later named, a wee thing blate
In their expression.

The prentit stanes that mark the deid,
Wi' lengthened lip, the sarious read;
Syne way a moraleesin' heid,
An then an' there
Their hirplin' practice an' their creed
Try hard to square.

It's here our Merren lang has lain,
A wee bewast the table-stane;
An' yon's the grave o' Sandy Blane;

An' further ower,
The mither's brithers, dacent men!
Lie a' the fower.

Here the guidman sall bide awee
To dwall amang the deid; to see
Auld faces clear in fancy's e'e;
Belike to hear
Auld voices fa'in saft an' slee
On fancy's ear.

Thus, on the day o' solemn things,
The bell that in the steeple swings
To fauld a scaittered faim'ly rings
Its walcome screed;
An' just a wee thing nearer brings
The quick an' deid.

But noo the bell is ringin' in;
To tak their places, folk begin;
The minister himsel' will shune
Be up the gate,
Filled fu' wi' clavers about sin
An' man's estate.

The tunes are up – FRENCH, to be shure,
The faithfu' FRENCH, an' twa-three mair;
The auld prezentor, hoastin' sair,
Wales out the portions,
An' yirks the tune into the air
Wi' queer contortions.

Follows the prayer, the readin' next,
An' than the fisslin' for the text –
The twa-three last to find it, vext
But kind o' proud;
An' than the peppermints are raxed,
An' southernwood.

For noo's the time whan pows are seen
Nid-noddin' like a mandareen;
When tenty mithers stap a preen
In sleepin' weans;
An' nearly half the parochine
Forget their pains.

There's just a waukrif' twa or three:
Thrawn commentautors sweer to `gree,
Weans glowrin' at the bumlin' bee
On windie-glasses,
Or lads that tak a keek a-glee
At sonsie lasses.

XXI

Himsel', meanwhile, frae whaur he cocks
An' bobs belaw the soundin'-box,
The treesures of his words unlocks
Wi' prodigality,
An' deals some unco dingin' knocks
To infidality.

XXII

Wi' snappy unction, hoo he burkes
The hopes o' men that trust in works,
Expounds the fau'ts o' ither kirks,
An' shaws the best o' them
No muckle better than mere Turks,
When a's confessed o' them.

XXIII

Bethankit! what a bonny creed!
What mair would ony Christian need? –
The braw words rumm'le ower his heid,
Nor steer the sleeper;

And in their restin' graves, the deid
Sleep aye the deeper.

And a note below on this poem by Louis:

'It may be guessed by some that I had a certain parish in my eye, and this makes it proper I should add a word of disclamation. In my time there have been two ministers in that parish. Of the first I have a special reason to speak well, even had there been any to think ill. The second I have often met in private and long (in the due phrase) 'sat under' in his church and neither here nor there have I heard an unkind or ugly word upon his lips. The preacher of the text had thus no original in that particular parish; but when I was a boy he might have been observed in many others; he was then (like the schoolmaster) abroad; and by recent advices, it would seem he has not yet entirely disappeared.'

Charles gives his own explanation as follows:

The church of which Louis wrote was the old parish church of North Berwick, now dismantled on the rising ground above the High Street.

The two ministers under which he sat were Revd Peter McMorland and the Revd Dr Sprott. Louis attended the church many a time. I sometimes sat with him in the loft or gallery, which was allocated to Sir Hew Dalrymple of Leuchie, opposite the pulpit. A smaller loft was given over to Sir George Grant-Suttie of Balgone whose family attended most regularly for many a long day.

The pews of the church were mostly long benches, but some were formed into squares with doors–these latter were allocated mostly to the people of the large farms in the parish; Wamphray, Congleton, Bonnington etc. The doors had the name of the various farms painted upon them. The square seats were a much more friendly arrangement for a family than the long bench seats.

Louis sometimes sat in the dark, oak-panelled loft where I generally was. We usually came into the churchyard by the small wicket gate in the 'lang loan benorth the kirkyard'. It's a dark bogle infested lane within the hand clutch I would say of the dead over the then low wall and 'besides that the church itself had always an Ill name since the days of James VI' and according to Louis 'the devil's cantrips (tricks) played therein when the Queen was on the seas'.

The minister was opposite this dismal den with the precentor 'David' below him, the minister adorned on each side of him by marble tablets of the dead, the sermons and prayers being dreary and the singing equally so. The only redeeming feature was the comely and smiling face of Sir George Grant-Suttie's younger daughter, with her kind and cheerful demeanour, although many years older than me, sitting in the gallery nearly opposite our den. The den was also free from the admixture of peppermint and the smell of humanity.

The Speculative Society

During Louis' second year at the College of Edinburgh, now called the University, he became a member of the Speculative Society. This was a society dear to his heart, being more or less a secret society, although I hasten to add nothing wrong took place there. No student ever went around asking anyone to join; really it was a friendship society. It was neither known by whom it was started nor when and not even what the members' privileges or rights were.

In one of my inspections, I couldn't see anything older than that of Sir Walter Scott's time. It seemed to me that the place needed a good clean out and paint. The room was desolate, dreary and the whole seemed veiled in mystery which no doubt suited Louis, as his pleasure throughout life was mystery. Long live the Speculative Society!

The hall of the Speculative Society in the University of Edinburgh.

A Dinner Speech

This is the address Louis made as his Edinburgh Academy Class Dinner
Club dinner speech for his final year:

Dear Thamson* class, whaure'er I gang
It aye comes ower me wi' a spang:
'LORDSAKE! THEY THAMSON LADS – (DEIL HANG
OR ELSE LORD MEND THEM!) –
AN' THAT WANCHANCY ANNUAL SANG**
I NE'ER CAN SEND THEM!'

Straucht, at the name, a trusty tyke,
My conscience girrs ahint the dyke;***
Straucht on my hinderlands I fyke
To find a rhyme t' ye;
Pleased – although mebbe no pleased-like –
To gie my time t'ye.

'WEEL,' an' says you, wi' heavin' breist,
'SAE FAR, SAE GUID but WHAT'S THE NEIST?
YEARLY WE GAITHER TO THE FEAST,
A' HOPEFU' MEN –
YEARLY WE SKELLOCH 'HANG THE BEAST –
NAE SANG AGAIN!'

My lads, an' what am I to say?
Ye shurely ken the Muse's way:
Yestreen, as gleg's a tyke – the day,
Thrawn like a cuddy:
Her conduc', that to her's a play,
Deith to a body.

Aft whan I sat an' made my mane,
Aft whan I laboured burd-alane*****

124

Fishin' for rhymes an' findin' nane,
Or nane were fit for ye –
Ye judged me cauld's a chucky stane –
No car'n' a bit for ye!

But saw ye ne'er some pingein' bairn
As weak as a pitaty-par'n' –
Less used wi' guidin' horse-shoe airn
Than steerin' crowdie*****
Packed aff his lane, by moss an' cairn,
To ca' the howdie.

Wae's me, for the puir callant than!
He wambles like a poke o' bran,
An' the lowse rein, as hard's he can,
Pu's, trem'lin' handit;
Till, blaff! upon his hinderlan'
Behauld him landit.

Sic-like – I awn the weary fac' –
Whan on my muse the gate I tak,
An' see her gleed e'e raxin' back
To keek ahint her; –
To me, the brig o' Heev'n gangs black
As blackest winter.

'LORDSAKE! WE'RE AFF,' thinks I, 'BUT WHAUR?
ON WHAT ABHORRED AN' WHINNY SCAUR,
OR WHAMMLED IN WHAT SEA O' GLAUR,
WILL SHE DESERT ME?
AN' WILL SHE JUST DISGRACE? OR WAUR –
WILL SHE NO HURT ME?'

Kittle the quaere! But at least
The day I've backed the fashious beast,
While she, wi' mony a spang an' reist,
Flang heels ower bonnet;

An' a' triumphant – for your feast,
Hae! there's your sonnet!

Again, below are some hints of explanation:

> *Thomson was the name of the master of Louis' class.
> **Each class at completion of school held a dinner at the end of their final year.
> ***Dyke is the name for a Scottish drystone wall.
> ****RLS was an only child.
> *****Crowdie is a Scottish dish of milk resembling cream cheese.

The Royal Society of Edinburgh

There were a great many distinguished members of the Royal Society including Lord Kevin, Sir Robert Christison, Professor Tait, Dr Buchan, Professor Keland, Professor Turner, Dr Hutton Balfour, David Stevenson, Dr Simpson and Professor Crum Brown. A vocal member, Mr Robertson, full of fun said at one of the society's meetings that mathematical division was just the same as multiplication and fractions and proceeded to the blackboard with a piece of chalk.

He rapidly filled the blackboard with many figures and a's and b's and x's and y's. When he got to the bottom, he paused a moment then put the symbol, which I suppose everyone in the room understood meant QED, which had to be demonstrated. Roars of laughter and applause followed for the magician who had given them this unusual treat. It needs to be understood as a rule not a sound was heard in the room, not even the sound of a pin's fall!

In making his presentation Mr Robertson was dressed in full evening dress, as Louis had been when making his own presentation. On occasion of this lecture Louis was not present, he only ever attended a few. It could be said Louis was now as a ship, set on an even keel and in perfect trim, ready for the voyage up the Ladder of Fame.

In Narrow Waters

Louis had walked from 17 Heriot Row to our house in Melville Street and, as usual, marched into the drawing room and with much formality presented a suitably inscribed copy of his book *Inland Voyage* to my father. Both of them must have remembered the 'History of Moses, and the march of the Israelites out of Egypt'. My father, his Uncle David, had offered a prize for the best essay from any one of the cousins, which Louis had duly won. Louis remembering this offer, was presenting his book in acknowledgement, providing evident pleasure for David and a symbol of satisfaction for both!

A few words jokingly made between them of plagiarism, owing to the likeness of title of their two books, David's *Canal and River Engineering* and Louis' *Inland Voyage,* the subject of both being in narrow water. Louis and David shared a good laugh about this coincidence.

Louis' Ladder of Fame

So much is known of Louis' creative writing in its many forms but before he had made his mark in this respect, there had been a more scientific side to the man.

Between the age of 21 and 24 years, Louis drafted papers to be read between the two principal societies of Edinburgh, namely the Royal Scottish Society of Arts and the Royal Society of Edinburgh. These papers would become steps in Louis' ladder of fame.

The first paper was a proposal by Louis to use a mirror revolving around a fixed light to produce an intermittent flash. So interesting was the paper that Louis was awarded the silver medal by the Royal Scottish Society of Arts.

The medal is and was a round and heavy piece of silver, reflecting well a worthy place in history, for it was the first step of recognition in Louis' ladder of fame. The reverse side of the medal was engraved with Louis' name, together with a description of the paper. The front of the medal was the image of Minerva – the Goddess of Wisdom, the emblem of the society.

Not long after this event, I was also fortunate enough to gain recognition by the Royal Scottish Society of Arts for an invention using the power of gas to be the motive power in turning off and on the gas supply, thus forming a flashing light at will. This form of invention was later supplied to buoys all across the world.

Louis' second paper was one providing information on the thermal influence of forests, read on 8th May 1873 before the Royal Society of Edinburgh, about two years after his engineering paper. By then Louis had ceased writing on engineering as such. This second paper was interesting to those who understand the subject. The council decided whether a paper should be read, with no favouritism shown, but it was to be delivered by the author attired in formal evening dress The paper included a 17-page frontispiece. Those who judged the papers for reading and publishing must have been gratified by their early recognition of Louis' talent upon the publication of his first book *Inland Voyage* in 1878, showing conclusively that they were right in their judgement. They had backed the right horse as it were!

Charles produced a diagram which he called a bird's eye view of Louis' literary works. This analytical assessment seems typical of Charles' scientific mind.

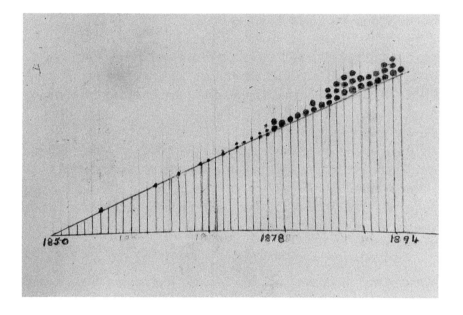

A glance at the diagram, on which Louis' works are depicted by dots, shows that even when Louis was at school, at university, then an apprentice at law, he was ever working and writing towards publication. Large black dots on the diagram mark his books. Clearly this illustrates that all had been changed as if by a magician's hand. From those early glorious days onwards, Louis wrote steadily at the rate of between one to three books every year until his death in 1894.

Charles also received a silver medal from the Royal Scottish Society of Arts.

*Louis, like his father before him, had a time when he was undecided
how he would proceed in life. After turning his back on engineering,
he studied law and indeed was called to the bar but never practised.
It seems clear that he would have regarded life as a lawyer as very dull.*

131

D. Alan Stevenson

Charles' son, known as Alan in the family, yet to the outside world was known as D. Alan to avoid confusion with his forebears. Realistically it never seemed likely he would have the opportunity to build lighthouses as such yet remained involved with lighthouses throughout his life.

Alan wrote two major books on lighthouses, as well as the authoritative reference book on Cape of Good Hope Triangular stamps. Like his father he was appointed to the Royal Company of Archers, the sovereign's bodyguard in Scotland.

The photograph is of D. Alan, with his wife Jessie and their son Quentin.

The Pharos of Alexandria

Charles decided not to write a piece directly about his son, Alan. However, Charles did include the following history about the Pharos lighthouse, which principally draws on Alan's research.

Perhaps the most famous early lighthouse was the Pharos of Alexandria, completed about 280 BC.

Pliny, the ancient Roman philosopher and military commander who died in 79AD, described the Pharos in detail. In a translation of 1601, it is referred to thus:

> *Over and above the Pyramids, another great construction is the tower built by one of the kings of Egypt within the Island Pharos and it keepeth and commandeth the haven of Alexandria, which tower they say cost eight hundred talents in its building. And here, because I would omit nothing worth the writing, I cannot but note the singular magnanimitie of kind Ptolome, who permitted Sostratus of Gnides (the master workman and architect) to engrave his own name on this building. The use of this watch-tower is to show light as a lanthorne (sic) and give direction in the night to ships, for to enter the haven and where they shall avoid barrs and shelves.*

Pliny adds that some mariners found the lighthouse misleading.

> *This is the danger only, lest when many lights in this lantern meet together, they should be taken for a star in the Skie, for that afar off such lights appears unto sailors in the manner of a star.*

Unlike Smeaton's Eddystone or the Stevenson family's lighthouses of Skerryvore, North Unst and Bell Rock, the Pharos stood on an island beyond the reach of any seas.

It is unclear how tall the Pharos tower was. Charles' son D. Alan Stevenson in his major book *The World's Lighthouses* before 1820, explained in detail that the height was estimated at 450 feet and had a base of around 100 feet square. This could provide a light with a visible range up to a maximum of 29 miles.

In his book he wrote,

> *The lantern on its top was destroyed about the 8th century but much of the tower survived in its original form until about 1200, when it was overthrown by an earthquake. The fact that it endured as a great mass of stone for more than 1,500 year gives the impression that it indeed may have been a structure even greater than the dimensions suggested by archaeologists.*

A Final Thought

Jean Leslie was one of the granddaughters of Charles Stevenson and through her own determination and with help from Roland Paxton she successfully published *Bright Lights*, a history of the Stevenson engineers. This included several mentions of material from Charles' *SCRAPS* manuscript. Jean showed much kindness to me over many years after the death of my mother, in 1966.

Jean Leslie and Nicholas Stevenson in front of a bust of Robert Stevenson. Nicholas is the son of Quentin and grandson of D. Alan Stevenson.

May Yeoman wanted to see the manuscript of *SCRAPS*, which she had worked on so diligently for Charles, brought to final publication. She explained this in a written instruction shortly before her death in 1972. I hope she would have been happy with the end result.

Roderick Groundes-Peace

Appendix

The rough draft of the planned frontispiece that Charles had started, and May Yeoman continued, as his writing was no longer legible.

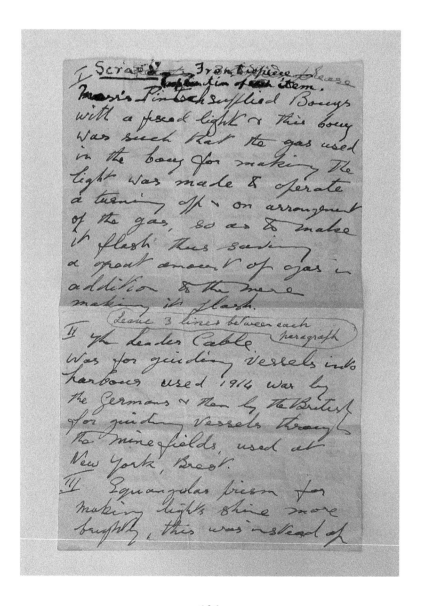

Fresnel's prism.

I The inaccessible
Fog-gun. This was used
at Roseneath Patch on
the Clyde. Marconie
admitted that they did
not know how to do it.

V the Combination of
Hyper-radiant & 1st order
apparatus, in one optical
apparatus to get maximum
candle power

VI the Electric Driven
Fog signal by Submarine
Cable as at Platte Fougere
Was a solitary example

VII Acetelyne Gas for explosion
was first used at Clyde.

VIII Broadcast of speech.
was first done by C.A.S.
(before anyone else) & transmit
Voice across space

King George and Queen Elizabeth Officers' Club
2 Castle Street, Edinburgh, 2
TELEPHONE 21632
HOSPITALITY AND INFORMATION BUREAU

Milton Keynes UK
Ingram Content Group UK Ltd.
UKHW040045071023
430092UK00002B/9/J